Roadmap to 3rd Grade Reading: VIRGINIA EDITION

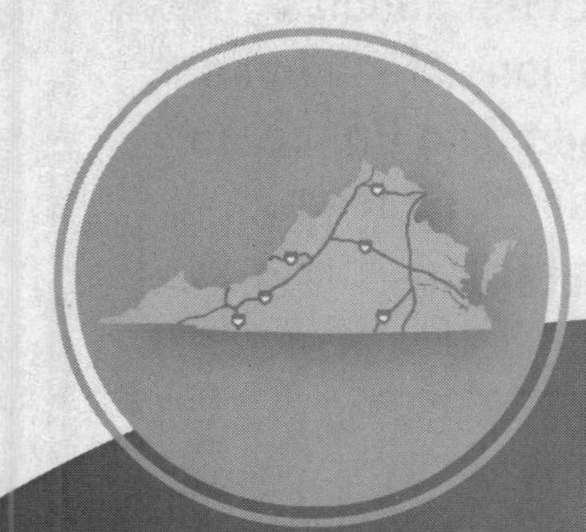

Roadmap to 3rd Grade Reading: VIRGINIA EDITION

by
Greg Faherty

Random House, Inc.
New York

www.review.com

This workbook was written by The Princeton Review, one of the nation's leaders in test preparation. The Princeton Review helps millions of students every year prepare for standardized assessments of all kinds. The Princeton Review offers the best way to help students excel on standardized tests.

The Princeton Review is not affiliated with Princeton University or Educational Testing Service.

Princeton Review Publishing, L.L.C.
160 Varick Street, 12th Floor
New York, NY 10013

E-mail: comments@review.com

Published in the United States by Random House, Inc., New York.

ISBN 0-375-75575-6

Editor: Russell Kahn
Development Editor: Rachael Nevins
Director of Production: Iam Williams
Design Director: Tina McMaster
Art Director: Neil McMahon
Production Manager: Mike Rockwitz
Ollie the Ostrich illustrated by Paulo De Freitas Jr.
Manufactured in the United States of America

9 8 7 6 5 4 3 2

First Edition

Contents

Parent/Teacher Introduction

About this Book

The Princeton Review is one of the nation's leaders in test preparation. We prepare more than 2 million students every year with our courses, books, online services, and software programs. In addition to helping Virginia students with their Standards of Learning (SOL) assessments, we coach students around the country on many other statewide standardized tests, as well as on college-entrance exams such as the SAT-I, SAT-II, PSAT, and ACT. Our strategies and techniques are unique and, most importantly, successful. Our goal is to reinforce skills that students have been taught in the classroom and to show them how to apply those skills to the specific format and structure of the Virginia SOL English: Reading Assessment for grade 3.

Roadmap to 3rd Grade Reading: Virginia Edition contains three basic elements: lessons, test-preparation, and practice tests. Each lesson (or "mile") focuses on a specific skill, such as finding the main idea and supporting details of a passage. The miles walk students through the basics in ways that emphasize active learning and boil down information into easily retained and recalled chunks. Each lesson is coupled with focused test-prep that encourages students to apply what they've learned in exercises. The book also contains three full-length practice tests. Each practice test is modeled after the actual Virginia SOL Grade 3 Reading Assessment in both style and content. This will help you assess which skills students should review and improve upon before they take the actual SOL Reading Assessment. It will also show you how much the students have improved after working on the lessons in this book. (Answer keys and explanations for the lessons and the practice tests are available beginning on page 167.)

We've also provided a Progress Chart as a way to encourage and motivate students. The Progress Chart is broken up into twenty-seven miles, along with seven review sections called map checks. It will help students see how far they've come in their preparation. Studying for any test can be difficult for young students, and it is as important to encourage good study habits as it is to remediate students' weaknesses. Be vigilant about reminding students how well they are doing and how much they've learned. Anxiety is their worst enemy. Building confidence goes a long way toward helping students succeed on any standardized test.

Before students begin their test preparation, take a moment to review the table of contents and to flip through the lessons in the book. We've tried to present the material in such a way that each skill presented builds on the previous one, but we realize that every student and every class has different strengths and weaknesses. There's no harm in students working on the lessons out of sequence.

About the Virginia Standards of Learning (SOL) English: Reading Assessment for Grade 3

All third-grade students in Virginia are required to take the Virginia SOL English Assessment. The test contains a reading and a writing section. This book focuses on the reading portion of the English assessment.

The reading test includes thirty-five multiple-choice questions. Ten of these questions will be field-test items that will not count toward students' scores. Because there is no way to differentiate the field-tested items from the scored items, students should answer all of the questions as if they count toward their scores. Students must choose one of four answer choices for each question. For each answer choice they select, they must fill in the corresponding bubble on the separate answer sheet provided.

Students' test scores are reported as either failing, proficient, or advanced. Students' SOL test scores in grades K–8 will be used as one factor in determining grade promotion or retention. In 2001 third-grade students passed the SOL English assessment only 65 percent of the time, making it the most troublesome SOL third-grade test. By 2007 schools risk losing their accreditation if less than 70 percent of their students pass the SOL exams.

Note: Check with the Virginia Department of Education for the most recent information about score reporting. Check with your school district for the test's administration date in your area.

The following Virginia Department of Education website has updates about the Virginia Standards of Learning:

http://www.pen.k12.va.us/VDOE/Instruction/sol.html

The Grade 3 English Test blueprints, which include a list of the standards assessed on the test, can be found at the following website:

http://www.pen.k12.va.us/VDOE/Assessment/soltests/eng3.html

Practical Notes for Testing Day

- Because there is no guessing penalty, students should answer all of the questions on the test. They should not leave questions unanswered because they find them difficult. (Students should review the test-taking technique Getting Rid of Wrong Answer Choices on pages 20 and 21 to improve their chances of correctly answering difficult questions.)

- The test is *untimed,* so students should not get anxious about finishing as quickly as possible.

- Remind students that they will have to use bubble sheets to record their answers. Tell them to check their places on the bubble sheets often so they don't fill in the right answer for the wrong question by accident. They should practice using the bubble sheets that precede each practice test in the book.

Nine Simple Things You Can Do to Help Students Read Better

1. Read to your students.

Read stories aloud to your students and then discuss the stories with them. Talk together about the characters and discuss what happens in the story, especially if the plot turns out to be surprising. You may want to have students read along with you, or ask them to locate words on the page.

2. Help your students read on their own.

Independent reading helps students to succeed in school. Help your students get their own library cards and let them pick out their own books. Suggest reading as a fun free-time activity.

3. Show your students why reading is important.

Explain to your students how reading plays a vital role in everyday life. Show how strong reading skills can help them with both practical (in driving, following directions, and reading receipts, bills, and contracts) and entertaining (reading newspapers, magazines, and books) aspects of life. Make sure your students set aside time during the day to read.

4. Make sure students have writing tools available.

Students generally want to learn how to read and write. Help them to do that by having paper, pencils, pens, or crayons available for them at all times. Work with them if they ask you to.

5. Set a good example.

Students learn from their parents and teachers. You can set a good example for them by reading newspapers, magazines, and books.

6. Supply books on tape for learning-disabled students.

Learning disabilities may frustrate young readers. Books on tape can be a terrific substitute for reading for learning-disabled readers. If you can't find books on tape for your students' favorite books, you can always record them yourself.

7. Track students' progress.

Create a system for students so that they can visualize their progress. It helps students to build confidence if they can see how they are improving their skills. The Progress Chart on page 8 is a great way to show students' progress through this book.

8. Ask students to tell you about events in their lives.

Describing the events and telling the stories that occur in their lives helps students learn about stories in general. It can also help them understand what the stories they read mean.

9. Use television as a tool.

Educational television programs have the power to teach students about many subjects. Try to restrict the use of noneducational television.

Student Introduction

About this Book

You probably don't like tests. Given the choice, you'd never take another test again, right? Well, this book makes it fun to learn how to take tests. This book includes games to play, puzzles to finish, pictures to draw, and questions to answer.

Every lesson in this book is a "mile" on a trip that helps you do your best on the Virginia SOL English: Reading Test. Each mile reviews a skill that you should know for the SOL test. We'll take you through all the basics in the miles. You can review your answers in the miles beginning on page 167. And after you review, you will get a chance to show what you know by taking a pratice test. What could be more fun than that?

Track how far you have come on the Progress Chart on page 8 by coloring in each mile after you've finished it. The Map Checks are places to stop, take a rest, and then try some new questions.

You'll be an expert at reading in no time at all. The only thing left will be for you to show your parents and teachers what you've learned by acing your SOL reading test. We've given you three complete practice tests. These practice tests can show you exactly how great your reading skills are!

You still might not like tests. That's okay. But by the time you get to the end of the *Roadmap to 3rd Grade Reading,* you'll be ready to do your best on them!

What Else Can I Do?

There are other things you can do to prepare for the SOL reading test.

- **Ask questions.** If you are confused after you finish a mile or a question, ask a parent or teacher for help. Asking questions is the best way to make sure that you understand what you have to in order to do your best!

- **Read.** Read everything you can. Read the newspaper, magazines, books, plays, poems, comics, and even the back of your cereal box. The more you read, the better you will be able to read. And the better you read, the more likely you are to do well on the SOL reading test. Reading more also helps you to become a better writer!

- **Learn new words.** Vocabulary is a big part of this test. The more words you know, the easier the test will seem. Try carrying index cards with you. Any time you come across a word you don't know, write it down. When you have time, look up the definition and write it on the back of the card. You can turn learning vocabulary into a game. Use your cards to test yourself. Set goals for learning new words every week. Ask teachers for help if you want. They can suggest some great new words for you to learn.

- **Eat well and get a good night's sleep.** Your body doesn't work well when you don't eat good food and get enough sleep. Neither does your brain. On the night before the test, make sure to go to bed at your normal time. You should also eat a healthy breakfast on the morning of the testing day. Nothing will help you do better than being awake and alert while taking the SOL reading test.

- **Get used to seeing numbered lines and paragraphs**. The SOL test puts numbers in front of every line of its poems and every paragraph of its stories. These aren't parts of the stories. The numbers are there to help you find a certain word or sentence. Some questions will even tell you to look at a certain line or paragraph to find an answer.

This is just the beginning of the road. There are great things to learn ahead. So buckle your seat belt and get ready to travel to the first mile toward reading excellence.

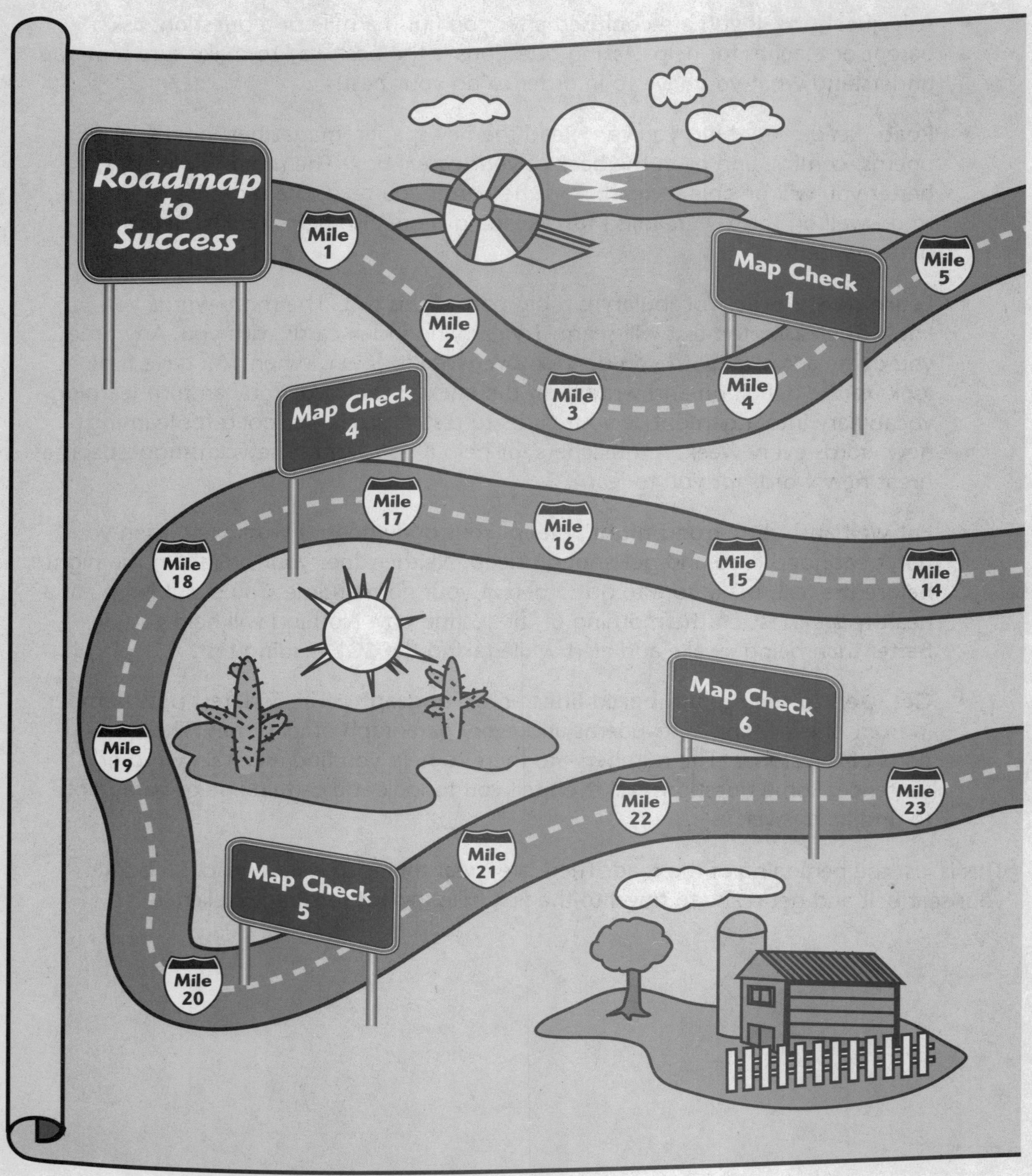
Roadmap to Success
Mile 1
Mile 2
Mile 3
Mile 4
Map Check 1
Mile 5
Map Check 4
Mile 17
Mile 16
Mile 15
Mile 14
Mile 18
Mile 19
Map Check 6
Mile 22
Mile 23
Mile 21
Map Check 5
Mile 20

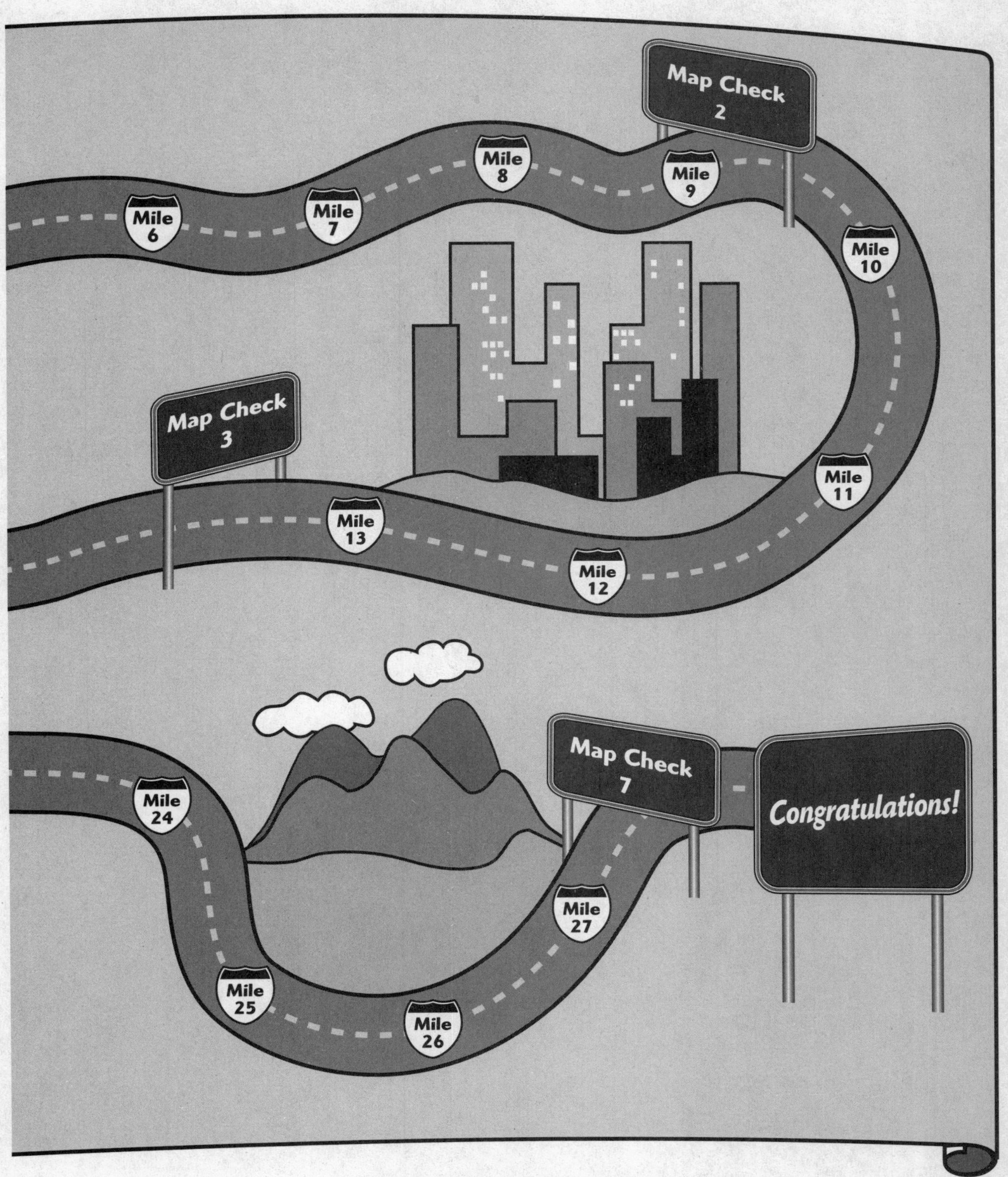
Map Check
2
Mile
6
Mile
7
Mile
8
Mile
9
Mile
10
Map Check
3
Mile
11
Mile
13
Mile
12
Map Check
7
Mile
24
Congratulations!
Mile
27
Mile
25
Mile
26

MILE BY MILE

MILE 1: WORD SOUNDS

Sometimes the same letter can have different sounds. For example the letter C sounds different in different words, such as "cat," "chalk," and "face." Always try to sound out words that are new to you so that you know how they are pronounced. Remember that vowel sounds use the letters A, E, I, O, U, and Y.

Directions: Circle the correct answer for each of the following twenty-two questions.

1 Here is a picture.

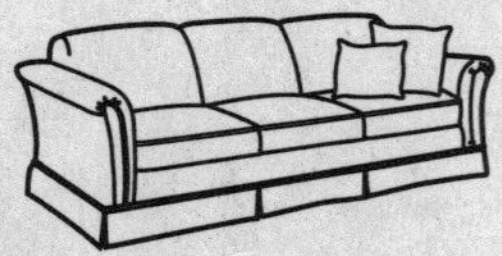

Which word below ends with the same sound as the name of the object in the picture above?

Push Lunch Crack

2 Here is a picture.

Which word below begins with the same sound as the name of the object in the picture?

Threw Chalk Phone

3 Here is a picture.

Which word below begins with the same sound as the name of the object in the picture above?

Garden Junk Age

4 Here is a picture.

Which word below has the same ending sound as the name of the animal in the picture?

Fib Can How

5 **Here is a picture.**

Which word below has the same beginning sound as the name of the object in the picture?

Catcher Picture Shadow

6 **Here is a picture.**

Which word below ends with the same ending sound as the name of the animal in the picture?

Wash House Crutch

7 **Here is a picture.**

Which word begins with the same sound as the beginning of the name of the object in the picture?

Charge Sheep Keep

8 **Here is a picture.**

Which word below begins with the same sound as the name of the object in the picture?

Chop Strength Sugar

9 **Here is a picture.**

Which word has the same ending sound as the name of the object above?

Sing Drink Laugh

10 **Here is a picture.**

Which word below has the same sound beginning and middle sounds as the name of the thing in the picture above?

Clue Town Cloud

11 **Here is a picture.**

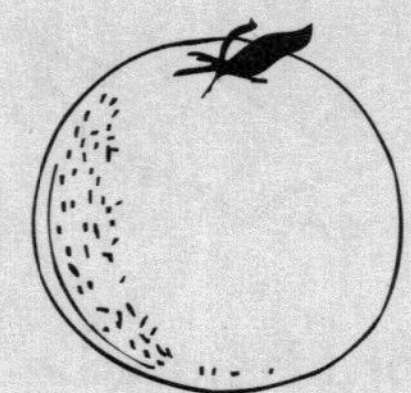

Which word ends with the same sound as the name of the fruit in the picture?

Drink Bang Strange

12 **Here is a picture.**

Which word has the same beginning sound as the name of the animal pictured above?

Zero Sheet Steam

13 **Here is a picture.**

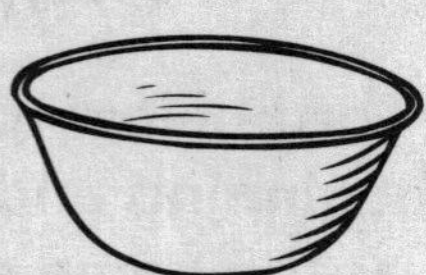

Which word has the same middle vowel sound as the name of the object in the picture above?

Stole Rule Spoon

14 **Here is a picture.**

Which of the following words has the same vowel sound as the name of the object in the picture?

Frog Luck Snag

15 **Here is a picture.**

Which of these words has the same vowel sound as the name of the object in the picture?

Seat Drink Bank

16 **Here is a picture.**

Which word has the same middle vowel sound as the name of the object in the picture?

Meat Move Nail

17 **Look at the picture below.**

Which word below has the same vowel and end sound as the name of the object in the picture?

Pond   Dream   Sand

18 **Look at the picture below.**

Which word has the same vowel sound as the name of the object in the picture?

Apple   Dinosaur   Team

19 **Look at the picture below.**

Which word has the same vowel sound as the name of the object in the picture?

High   Tall   Flip

20 **Look at the picture below.**

Which word has the same vowel and ending sound as the name of the object in the picture?

Rip   Mess   Hiss

21 **Look at the picture below.**

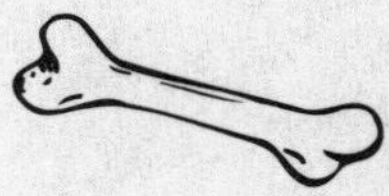

Which of the following words has the same vowel sound as the name of the object in the picture?

Own   Dine   Cool

22 **Look at the picture below.**

Which of these words ends with the same sound as the name of the object in the picture?

Fire   Fur   Fish

Mile 2: Rhyme

Many words **rhyme** with each other. That means that they end with the same sounds. Some rhyming words may be spelled similarly, like *boy* and *toy*. Other rhyming words may be spelled differently, like *shoe* and *true*.

Words that rhyme:	car/far	think/sink	treat/meet
Words that do not rhyme:	work/job	star/sky	trick/trip

Poems often include words that rhyme at the end of each line, or every other line.

Directions: Read the poem below about pets. Look for the words that rhyme.

Pets

Little kids and little pets
go together so well.
It doesn't matter where they live,
kids think pets are swell.

Dogs and cats, big and small,
oh yes, they are so fun.
Bunnies, birds, and even frogs:
pets are number one.

It doesn't matter where you live,
in a city or a farm.
Just remember this one rule,
pets you should not harm.

Every boy and every girl
wants to have a pet.
But the pets need food and love,
this you can't forget!

Directions: Look back at the poem you just read. Some of the lines end in words that rhyme with other words in the poem. Write down the numbers of the lines that rhyme with each other. The first one has been done for you.

1 The last word in line 2 rhymes with the last word in line ___4___.

2 The last word in line 10 rhymes with the last word in line ________.

3 The last word in line 14 rhymes with the last word in line ________.

Use the following list of words to answer the next four questions.

Fun	Toe	Dove	Call

Here is a line from the poem: "go together so well"

4 What word rhymes with go? ________

Here is a line from the poem: "Dogs and cats, big and small"

5 What word rhymes with small? ________

Here is a line from the poem: "pets are number one"

6 What word rhymes with one? ________

Here is a line from the poem: "But the pets need food and love"

7 What word rhymes with love? ________

Read the words below from the poem. Then write your own word that rhymes with each one.

Word

8 Rule ____________

9 Cat ____________

10 Farm ____________

Mile 3: Homophones

Sometimes two or more words sound the same but have different meanings and spellings. Think about the words *sun* and *son*. You pronounce both words the same way, but they don't mean the same thing. The *sun* is the star that warms and lights Earth. A *son* is a male child. Words like these are *homophones.* You will need to know some common homophones when you are writing.

Directions: Each sentence below has a blank line where a homophone should go. Circle the correct homophone from the pair that follows the sentence.

1 Mr. Lewis reads his children a ________ every night before bed. (tale, tail)

2 Mary's favorite vacation was spent at a beach house near the ________. (see, sea)

3 Darla was afraid to get stung by a ________. (be, bee)

4 Omar likes ____________ vegetables, but not others. (some, sum)

5 The teacher ____________ like to meet us after class. (wood, would)

Read each sentence below. Each one has an underlined word. Choose the homophone for the underlined word from the box on the bottom of the page. Write it on the line after the sentence.

6 The hunter <u>blew</u> his horn to start the foxhunt. ____________

7 It is time <u>to</u> go to school. ____________

8 Our book report is <u>due</u> tomorrow. ____________

9 Sometimes Ralph forgets to close his mouth when he <u>chews</u> his food. ____________

10 <u>I</u> need to find my boots. ____________

Two	Eye	Do	Choose	Blue

Directions: Read the following selections. When you see a pair of homophones, circle the one that belongs in that sentence.

11 **Jorge looked at Donnel and smiled. He (knew, new) that summer vacation was about to begin. Now that both boys were twelve, they could ride their bikes to the lake. Jorge had (herd, heard) that you could catch bass and trout (there, their), as well as bullfrogs. Both boys had saved some money to (by, buy) new fishing poles. Summer was going to begin in only an (our, hour)!**

12 **Lars looked at his watch. They were running late, and it was his sister's fault. Ingrid was always late. Now Lars (would, wood) have to look for her. First, he looked in her room. As usual, it was a mess. The bed was not (maid, made), and clothes were on the floor. Next, he looked in the living room and the kitchen. He searched the (hole, whole) house, but Ingrid was nowhere to be (seen, scene). Finally, he found her in the garage. By then, it was too late to catch the bus. Now they would have to wait until next (week, weak) to go see their cousin.**

Mile 4: Answering Multiple-Choice Questions

Each question on the SOL reading test has four answer choices. Imagine how much easier it would be if there were only two or three answer choices. Even if you weren't sure which answer choice was correct, you'd have a much better chance of picking the right one. Getting rid of wrong answer choices can make taking the test easier. Questions will be easier because there will be fewer answer choices from which to choose. Sometimes you can get rid of wrong answer choices as soon as you read them. Look at the following example. The passage is missing. Still, which answer choice can you get rid of right away?

► **In the story the author talks about how catfish use their fins to help them do what?**

○ **A** keep themselves cool in the summer

○ **B** swim along the bottom of streams

○ **C** hide from bigger fish

○ **D** catch and throw a baseball

Even though you have not read the story about catfish, you can be sure that they don't play baseball! Cross out choice **D.** Let's try another example.

► **What is Manny MOST LIKELY to do with his quarter?**

○ **F** buy a toy

○ **G** buy an apple

○ **H** buy a house

○ **J** buy a car

Look at the answer choices. Can you get rid of any of them? Manny might buy a toy with his quarter, so let's keep answer choice **A** for now. Can Manny buy an apple with his quarter? Maybe. Let's save that answer choice too. Can Manny buy a house with his quarter? No, houses cost much more than twenty-five cents! We can get rid of **C.** Can Manny buy a car? No, cars are very expensive and only adults can buy them, so answer choice **D** is wrong. We can get rid of that choice too.

Even without knowing the correct answer, there are only two possible answer choices to pick from. That means you have a better chance of picking the correct answer choice. If you can get rid of wrong answer choices, you can improve your score on any multiple-choice test!

Directions: Now it's your turn to practice getting rid of wrong answer choices. Read the following paragraph and then answer the questions that follow it. As you answer the questions, get rid of as many wrong answer choices as you can.

Drew and Cindy were late for school again. As usual, it was Drew's fault. The alarm clock was in Drew's room, and he slept through the alarm at least three times a week. Cindy would get ready as fast as she could, but it was usually too late. Cindy was worried because her teacher said if she was late again, a note would be sent home to their parents. She told Drew, but he just laughed. Drew never seemed to get worried. When she got to her class, Cindy's teacher, Ms. Lopez, handed Cindy a note and told her to bring it home. Cindy was very upset. It was Drew's fault that they were late, but she was going to get in trouble. It was not fair! On the way home, she didn't even talk to her brother. When Drew and Cindy's parents came home from work, Cindy handed them the note. She waited while they read it, ready to explain herself. After reading the note, Cindy's father yelled, "Drew! Come here! We need to talk about why you keep making your sister late for school!"

► **Why are Drew and Cindy late for school so often?**

○ **A** Cindy takes too long to get ready.

○ **B** Drew sleeps through his alarm.

○ **C** The bus driver forgets to pick them up.

○ **D** Ms. Lopez gives them the wrong directions.

Look at the passage to decide which answer choices are wrong. The paragraph never mentions a bus driver, so you can get rid of **C.** The paragraph also never mentions Ms. Lopez giving directions, so **D** is wrong too. Now there are only two choices left. If you read the first few sentences, you'll see that the correct answer is **B.**

Whenever you have a multiple-choice question, you should first try to get rid of as many wrong answer choices as you can. Then go back and choose from the ones that are left.

MAP CHECK 1

Directions: Read the story below about Karl and his lemonade stand. Then answer the questions that follow. As you answer the questions, try to get rid of wrong answer choices.

Karl and His Lemonade

1 Karl sat behind a large wooden box. The sign on the front of the box said COLD LEMONADE $1. Karl was upset. It seemed like no one wanted to buy any lemonade. He could not understand it. The weather was warm. It was a Saturday. He should have had a long line at his stand by now. Last summer his friend Toby had made twelve dollars in one day selling lemonade. Karl wanted to buy new sneakers. He had been saving his allowance all year. He only needed twenty more dollars to have enough money. Karl looked at his watch and decided that he would try for another hour, and then he would go home.

2 One hour later Karl still had not sold a single glass of lemonade. He stood up and started to put away the paper cups and ice. He would have to find another way to make the money he needed. He wondered if he could do some chores for money. Just then a man came running around the corner. He was wearing jogging pants, a sweaty red shirt, and yellow sneakers. He looked very thirsty. "Hey mister," said Karl. "Would you like to buy a cold glass of lemonade?" The man smiled, and he told Karl that he would.

3 After the man drank his lemonade, he winked at Karl and said, "You had better make some more lemonade, kid. I think you're going to be really busy in a few minutes." Then he jogged down the street. Karl looked back the other way and saw at least twenty people jogging toward him. They all looked hot and thirsty. Talk about luck! Now he would have enough money to buy his sneakers!

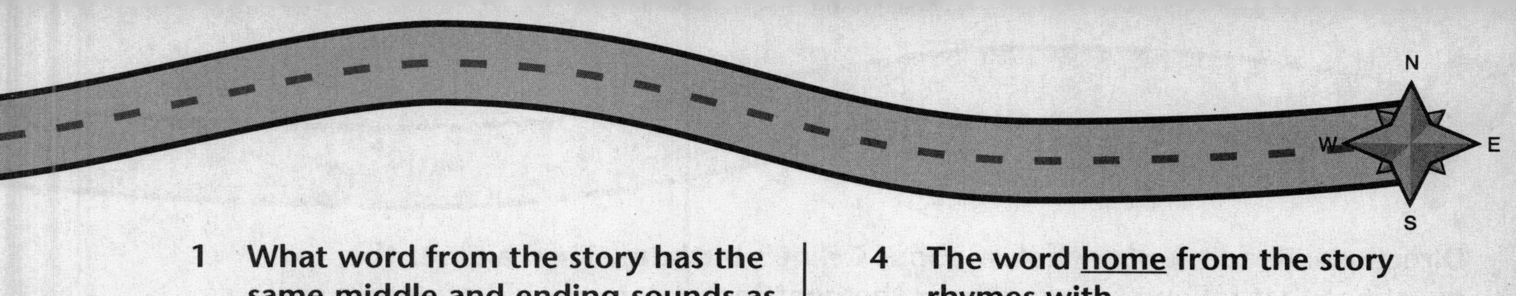

1 **What word from the story has the same middle and ending sounds as the word <u>sister</u>?**

- ○ **A** cents
- ○ **B** joggers
- ○ **C** mister
- ○ **D** sneakers

2 **Look at this picture.**

Which word from the story rhymes with the name of the objects in the picture?

- ○ **F** Karl
- ○ **G** watch
- ○ **H** sign
- ○ **J** box

3 **Look at the two sentences below.**

> **Karl is selling lemonade by the _____. He needs to make money for a new _____ of sneakers.**

Choose the correct pair of words to fill in the blank spaces above.

- ○ **A** rode, pair
- ○ **B** road, pear
- ○ **C** road, pair
- ○ **D** rode, pear

4 **The word <u>home</u> from the story rhymes with —**

- ○ **F** drone
- ○ **G** stain
- ○ **H** comb
- ○ **J** frown

5 **Look at this line from the story.**

> **The <u>sign</u> on the front of the box said COLD LEMONADE $1.**

Which of these words rhymes with <u>sign</u>?

- ○ **A** line
- ○ **B** bind
- ○ **C** some
- ○ **D** crying

6 **Look at this line from the story.**

> **Last summer his <u>friend</u> Toby had made twelve dollars in one day selling lemonade.**

Which of these words rhymes with <u>friend</u>?

- ○ **F** find
- ○ **G** bond
- ○ **H** send
- ○ **J** dent

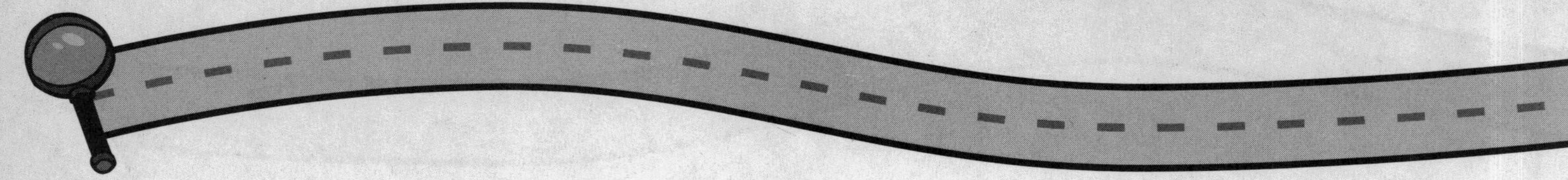

Directions: Read the story below about Celine's birthday. Then answer the questions that follow. As you answer the questions, try to get rid of wrong answer choices.

Celine's Birthday Present

1 Everyone clapped as Celine blew out the candles on her cake. "Did you make a wish?" her mother asked.

2 "Yes, but I know it will not come true," said Celine with a sad face. She sat in her chair while her mother served cake to the family. Celine wanted to open her presents, but she knew she had to wait. Finally, everyone was finished with the cake.

3 "Can I open my presents now?" she asked her parents.

4 "Go ahead," said her father. "Here, open this one first. It is from me and your mother." He handed her a large box covered in pretty wrapping paper. It had a large bow on the top.

5 Celine opened her present and screamed. "I can't believe it," she cried. "My very own art set. I can't wait to use it!" Celine's parents knew that Celine had seen the art set in a store, but she thought it was too expensive. They were glad they had been able to surprise her. Celine opened up the art set. Inside were colored pencils and pens, drawing paper, and an instruction book.

6 Celine's parents looked at each other and smiled. They could tell that Celine was happy because of her big grin. "Now we want you to draw us a beautiful picture that we can hang on the refrigerator," Celine's father told his daughter.

7 "I'm going to draw more than one," said Celine. "I will draw one for you, one for Mother, and one for Grandma." Celine took out the pencils and paper, and she walked over to the kitchen table. She left all of her other presents behind.

8 "Where are you going?" asked her mother.

9 "I am going to start drawing," Celine said. "After all, I have a lot of pictures to draw!" Everyone at the birthday party laughed.

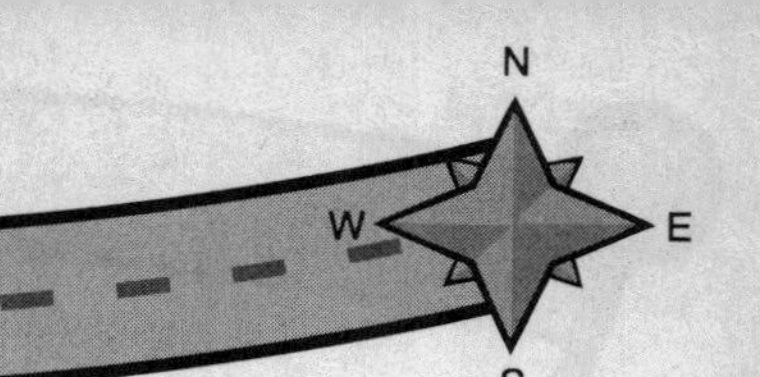

7 **Look at these two sentences about Celine and her family.**

Celine is _______ years old today. She has _______ brother and two sisters.

Fill in the blanks by choosing the correct pair of words from the choices below.

- ○ **A** ate, won
- ○ **B** eight, one
- ○ **C** ate, one
- ○ **D** eight, won

8 **Look at this picture.**

Which word from the story rhymes with the object in the picture?

- ○ **F** book
- ○ **G** store
- ○ **H** knew
- ○ **J** cried

9 **What word from the story has the same middle sound as teeth?**

- ○ **A** picture
- ○ **B** present
- ○ **C** smiled
- ○ **D** screamed

10 **The word art from the story rhymes with —**

- ○ **F** dart
- ○ **G** rat
- ○ **H** crate
- ○ **J** ate

11 **Here is a picture.**

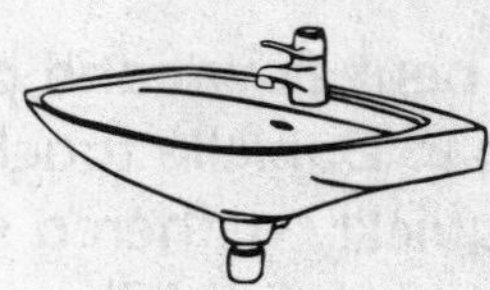

Which word from the story begins with the same sound as the object above?

- ○ **A** expensive
- ○ **B** inside
- ○ **C** Celine
- ○ **D** pencils

Directions: Read the story below about Danielle and her fantastic model airplane. Then answer the questions that follow. As you answer the questions, try to get rid of wrong answer choices.

Danielle's Model Airplane Contest

1 Danielle woke up and looked at her clock. It was seven o'clock in the morning. Danielle did not always get up this early, but today was special. She was too excited to sleep. Today was the model airplane contest. Danielle had spent three months building her plane. Danielle was going to get to fly it in her first contest. There would be many other people flying planes. Danielle knew she would have to do very well if she wanted to win.

2 Danielle ate breakfast with her family. They all wished her good luck. Her father said not to be afraid, but Danielle was. Her hands were shaking so badly that she almost spilled her juice. After breakfast, Danielle went into the garage. She checked her plane to make sure everything was okay. Then she went back into the house to wait. She tried to watch television, but she could not pay attention. Soon it was time to go. Danielle and her father put the plane in the car. Danielle and her parents drove to the park.

3 There were many different people flying their planes. Danielle knew that she could beat some of the other planes. Some other planes looked much better than hers. Finally, it was Danielle's turn to fly. She picked up her plane and walked out to the middle of the field.

4 Danielle bent down and pushed the starter button. The model airplane started up with a roar. Danielle touched the controls and the plane started to roll forward. It quickly gathered speed and took off. The plane flew up into the air faster than a bird. Danielle gently moved the controls, making the plane turn left and right. She aimed the plane straight up, and then straight down. Everyone watching thought it was going to crash. Just before it hit the ground, Danielle pushed the controls all the way up and the plane zoomed back into the air. Everyone clapped and cheered. Danielle flew the plane in a big circle, and then she landed it. The judges came over to her and said that she had won first prize!

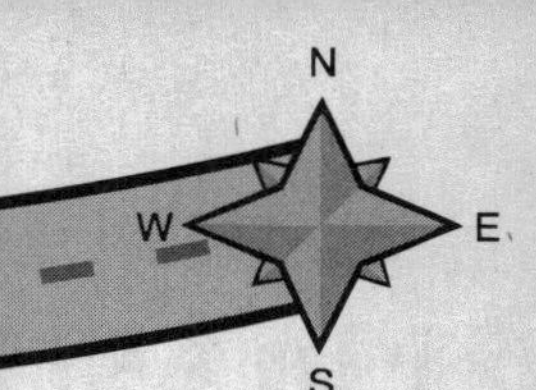

12 Look at this line from the story.

> Danielle knew she could <u>beat</u> some of the other planes.

Which of these words rhymes with <u>beat</u>?

- ○ **F** stream
- ○ **G** might
- ○ **H** rate
- ○ **J** feet

13 What word from the story has the same middle sound as <u>sore</u>?

- ○ **A** roar
- ○ **B** air
- ○ **C** bird
- ○ **D** ground

14 Look at this picture.

Which word from the story has the same ending sound as the object in the picture?

- ○ **F** fire
- ○ **G** turn
- ○ **H** told
- ○ **J** bag

15 Look at these two sentences.

> Danielle is flying a model ________. She ________ it herself in the garage.

Fill in the blanks by choosing the correct pair of words from the choices below.

- ○ **A** plain, made
- ○ **B** plain, maid
- ○ **C** plane, made
- ○ **D** plane, maid

16 The word <u>crash</u> from the story rhymes with —

- ○ **F** fast
- ○ **G** grass
- ○ **H** smash
- ○ **J** cage

17 Look at this line from the story.

> The judges came over to her and said she had won first <u>prize</u>.

Which of these words rhymes with <u>prize</u>?

- ○ **A** wise
- ○ **B** pitch
- ○ **C** less
- ○ **D** cross

Mile 5: Nouns, Verbs, Adjectives, and Adverbs

Words can do many things in a sentence. Some words show an action that happens. Some words help to describe other words. Here are four types of words that you should know. **Singular** words tell about one thing. **Plural** words tell about two or more things.

Noun: *Nouns* name a person, place, or thing. *Nouns* can be singular or plural.

Examples of nouns: <u>milk</u>, <u>party</u>, <u>John</u>, <u>dogs</u>, and <u>houses</u>.

Verb: An *action verb* shows action.

Examples of action verbs: <u>push</u> the door, she <u>swims</u>, <u>jump</u> high, and <u>climb</u> the hill.

Adjective: *Adjectives* describe *nouns*. They tell what kind or how many.

Examples of adjectives: <u>blue</u> sky, <u>warm</u> water, <u>cold</u> milk, and <u>many</u> people.

Adverb: *Adverbs* describe *verbs* or *adjectives*. They tell how, where, or when an action takes place.

Examples of adverbs: yelled <u>loudly</u>, ran <u>quickly</u>, and ate <u>slowly</u>.

Directions: Read each paragraph. Certain words are underlined. For each underlined word, tell whether it is a noun, verb, adjective, or adverb. Write your answer on the line next to the word. The first example has been done for you.

Elisa <u>walked</u> <u>slowly</u> down the <u>hall</u>. She heard the first <u>bell</u> <u>ring</u> <u>loudly</u> over her head. She was worried about her math test. Last night, when she should have been studying, she had made cookies instead. She needed to study, but she wanted some cookies. Nothing is better than <u>warm</u> <u>cookies</u>, fresh from a <u>hot</u> <u>oven</u>. The <u>moist</u> cookies had <u>melted</u> in her <u>mouth</u>. By the time she remembered to study, it had been time for bed. Now she was not ready for the <u>big</u> test.

1. walked *verb*
2. slowly ____________
3. hall ____________
4. bell ____________
5. ring ____________
6. loudly ____________
7. warm ____________
8. cookies ____________
9. hot ____________
10. oven ____________
11. moist ____________
12. melted ____________
13. mouth ____________
14. big ____________

The boat rocked gently on the rolling waves. The tall mast creaked in the breeze. Overhead a hot, yellow sun shone down on the ocean. Once in a while, a seagull would fly by, white feathers shining in the sunlight. No clouds disturbed the beautiful, blue sky. Suddenly, a door opened on the boat and a man came out onto the deck. He walked quickly to the back of the boat and started the engine. It roared to life, shattering the silence. The boat raced off and soon was gone from sight. All was quiet again.

15. boat ________
16. rocked ________
17. gently ________
18. rolling ________
19. waves ________
20. tall ________
21. mast ________
22. hot ________
23. yellow ________
24. sun ________
25. white ________
26. feathers ________
27. deep ________
28. blue ________
29. sky ________
30. walked ________
31. quickly ________
32. shattering ________

Trent opened the old door and peeked inside. The closet was dark and dusty. Old clothes hung on rusty wire hangers. Trent looked down at the closet floor. There was the black trunk that he had been looking for. His mother had asked him to get it. Inside it was a special gift for his birthday that she had been hiding all year. Trent leaned forward slowly to open the trunk with shaky fingers.

33. old ________
34. door ________
35. closet ________
36. dark ________
37. dusty ________
38. black ________
39. trunk ________
40. asked ________
41. special ________
42. gift ________
43. leaned ________
44. slowly ________
45. shaky ________
46. fingers ________

Mile 6: Prefixes and Suffixes

Prefixes are attached to the beginnings of words. They change the meaning of a word. By itself a prefix is not complete word. Look at the examples of prefixes below. See how they change the meanings of the words they are attached to.

Base Word	Meaning	Prefix	New Word	New Meaning
Build	to make	re-	rebuild	to make again
Happy	in a good mood	un-	unhappy	in a bad mood
Trust	to believe someone	dis-	distrust	to not believe someone

Directions: Below is a list of prefixes and base words. Use the prefixes and base words in the box to correctly fill in the blanks in the paragraph. The first example has been done for you.

Prefixes:	un-	dis-	un-	re-	in-
Base Words:	lucky	complete	belief	start	did

Diego stared in <u>disbelief</u> at the dinosaur. It roared loudly and walked toward him. Along the way, it crushed an __________ bush with its large feet. As it got closer, Diego saw that the dinosaur's left arm was __________, missing its hand. Just then the dinosaur stopped moving. A woman walked over to the dinosaur. She __________ a panel on the dinosaur's shin and fixed a loose wire. Then she shut the panel. She then hit a button on a remote control to __________ the dinosaur. The dinosaur started moving again. Soon the museum's new display would be complete.

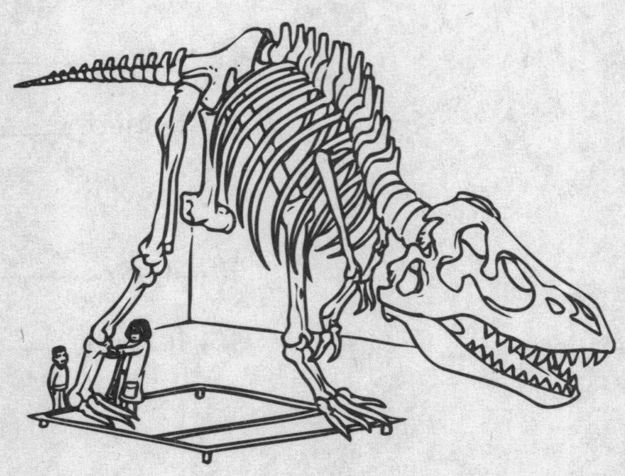

Suffixes are attached to the ends of words. They change the meaning of a word. By itself a suffix is not a complete word. Look at the examples of suffixes below. See how they change the meaning of the words they are attached to.

Base Word	Meaning	Suffix	New Word	New Meaning
Build	to make	-er	builder	someone who builds
Happy	in a good mood	-ly	happily	done in a happy way
Trust	to believe	-ful	trustful	full of trust
Taste	to have a flavor	-less	tasteless	having no taste
Confess	to admit guilt	-or	confessor	someone who confesses
Hug	to squeeze	-able	huggable	able to be hugged
Fear	to be afraid	-less	fearless	having no fear

Directions: Below is a list of suffixes and base words. Use the suffixes and base words in the box to correctly fill in the blanks in the paragraph.

Base Words:	hope	reuse	paint	peace	quick
Suffixes:	-able	-ly	-er	-less	-ful

Michelle looked into the living room. Her dog, Fredo, was asleep on the couch. He looked so ___________. She decided to take a picture of him. She got her camera out of the closet, but the film had no pictures left. Michelle wished that someone would invent ___________ film. She sat down to watch a television show about art. A ___________ was teaching people about colors. Michelle had tried to paint in art class, but she thought she was ___________. She ___________ changed the channel to something she liked better.

Mile 7: Contractions

A **contraction** is a word formed by putting two words together. The contraction is shorter than the original two words. The second word often loses a few letters when the two words make a contraction. An **apostrophe** shows where letters were lost before the words were joined.

Examples of contractions

I + will = I'll	We + will = We'll	They + will = They'll
I + am = I'm	We + are = We're	They + are = They're
Could + have = Could've	Should + have = Should've	Would + have = Would've
Could + not = Couldn't	Should + not = Shouldn't	Would + not = Wouldn't
It + is = It's	Have + not = Haven't	He + is = He's

Directions: Read the section below. After each underlined contraction, write the two words used to make it.

Wei-Lin looked at his watch. He knew he shouldn't (1.) __________ be awake, but he couldn't (2.) __________ sleep. He was too excited. In just a few hours, he and his brother would be leaving for summer camp. This was going to be Wei-lin's first trip to camp. For the past two years he had been wishing he could've (3.) __________ gone to camp like his brother. Now he was finally old enough. Wei-Lin didn't (4.) __________ think he would be able to sleep at all tonight. He lay on his pillow, thinking if there was anything else he should've (5.) __________ packed. He had clothes, a toothbrush, some money, and a compass. The camp would supply everything else. As he thought about camp, he slowly fell asleep.

Wei-Lin woke up when his brother Cho came into the room. "Wake up and get dressed, or we'll (6.) __________ be late!" he yelled at Wei-Lin. Wei-Lin jumped out of bed and got dressed as fast as he could.

"Maybe they'll (7.) __________ leave without me," he thought to himself. He grabbed his bag and ran downstairs.

"It's (8.) __________ about time," Cho said. "The bus is going to be here any minute."

"I'm (9.) __________ really going to camp," Wei-Lin said with a smile. "This will be the best summer I've (10.) __________ ever had!"

Directions: Read the section below. For each pair of underlined words, write the contraction that the two words form when joined.

Anna opened the door and entered the doctor's office. She went to the window and told the nurse her name. "Where is (11.)__________ your mother?" asked the nurse.

"She is (12.)__________ coming," said Anna. "She is having trouble with my little brother, Jon. He is (13.)__________ afraid of doctors."

The nurse smiled and said, "Lots of children are afraid of doctors. Why are not (14.)__________ you?"

"I do not (15.)__________ mind coming to the doctor's office," replied Anna. "I think it is (16.)__________ very interesting. When I grow up, I would (17.)__________ like to be a doctor."

Just then Anna's mother came in with Jon. His face was all red. Anna could tell he had (18.)__________ been crying. Anna did not know why her brother was afraid. They were only going to get their annual check-ups. They would not (19.)__________ even have to worry about getting a shot. Dr. Rocco was a nice lady. She always gave Anna a lollipop when they were done. Sometimes Dr. Rocco gave Anna an extra lollipop to give to Jon. "Maybe next time he will (20.)__________ be less afraid," she would tell Anna.

Anna's mother sat down next to Anna. She gave Jon some toys to play with. "I wish he would (21.)__________ learn to enjoy these visits like you do," said Anna's mother.

"Maybe he will (22.)__________ be braver next year," said Anna.

Mile 8: Abbreviations

An **abbreviation** is a way to write certain words so that they are shorter. An abbreviation ends with a period. Abbreviations are often capitalized. Look at the examples below.

Titles before names:	Mister = Mr.	Reverend = Rev.	Doctor = Dr.
Days of the week:	Sunday = Sun.	Friday = Fri.	Monday = Mon.
Months of the year:	January = Jan.	August = Aug.	February = Feb.

Directions: Each sentence below has an underlined abbreviation in it. At the end of each sentence is a blank line. Write the full word for each abbreviation on the blank line. The first example has been done for you.

1 **I have to go to the dentist on <u>Tues</u>. afternoon.** Tuesday

2 **<u>Mr</u>. Hedaya owns the bakery in town.** ____________

3 **Our house is located on Main <u>St</u>.** ____________

4 **People think <u>Rev</u>. Simons is helpful.** ____________

5 **My birthday is on <u>Sept</u>. third.** ____________

6 **<u>Thurs</u>. is the last day of school.** ____________

7 **Last <u>Wed</u>. my parents bought a new television.** ____________

8 **People say that <u>Jan</u>. is the coldest month.** ____________

9 **<u>Dr</u>. Rocco gave me a lollipop when I went to her office.** ____________

10 **My family likes to go to the movies every <u>Fri</u>. night.** ____________

11 **Every <u>Mon</u>. we get milk delivered to our house.** ____________

12 **Orchard <u>Ave</u>. is three blocks from here.** ____________

13 **We are going to visit my grandparents in <u>Feb</u>.** ____________

14 **Our paperboy is often late with the <u>Sat</u>. newspaper.** ____________

Mile 9: Who Owns It?

An apostrophe followed by the letter s at the end of a noun can show that something belongs to that person or thing. A singular noun, such as *boy,* becomes *boy's* to show that something belongs to him. *Boy's* is a possessive noun. Look at the examples below.

Roy's house is blue. **The dog's bone is in the kitchen.** **A tree's leaves fall off in the fall.**

Sandy's new bike is nice. **The car's tire was flat.** **Mitsy's paws were white.**

Directions: Each of the following sentences includes an underlined noun. Rewrite the noun as a possessive noun on the blank line in the new sentence. The first one has been done for you.

1	**The house that belongs to Mary is red.**	**Mary's house is red.**
2	**My brother has a new coat.**	**My __________ coat is new.**
3	**That book belongs to Daddy.**	**That is __________ book.**
4	**Those roller skates belong to Mia.**	**Those are __________ roller skates.**
5	**The waves of the ocean were high.**	**The __________ waves were high.**
6	**The movie has jokes that are funny.**	**The __________ jokes are funny.**
7	**That snake has pretty colors.**	**The __________ colors are pretty.**
8	**Did you bring the homework of Mike?**	**Did you bring __________ homework?**
9	**Does the whistle of the train still blow?**	**Does the __________ whistle still blow?**
10	**The tie Harvey has is new.**	**__________ tie is new.**
11	**What do the whiskers of a cat do?**	**What do a __________ whiskers do?**
12	**The ink of the pen is blue.**	**The __________ ink is blue.**
13	**The handle of the phone is broken.**	**The __________ handle is broken.**
14	**A button on my shirt is missing.**	**My __________ button is missing.**
15	**Sheila has a plant that is tall.**	**__________ plant is tall.**

MAP CHECK 2

Directions: Read this story about a young boy. Then answer the questions that follow.

Omar the Invisible Boy

1 "I wish I were invisible!" cried Peter.

2 His sister, Mandy, looked at him and shook her head. "You should be careful what you wish for," said Mandy seriously. "It might come true."

3 "Why would that be bad?" asked Peter. He closed his schoolbooks with a slam. "If I were invisible, I wouldn't have to do my homework."

4 "You think being invisible would be fun? Let me tell you a story about a little boy who became invisible."

5 Peter sat up in his chair as Mandy began her story.

6 "Once there was a boy named Omar. Omar did not like to do his chores. Omar wished he could be invisible. One day while he was sweeping the floor, a genie appeared. 'I have been listening to you,' said the genie, 'and I have decided to grant you your wish.' Omar could not believe his good luck. He closed his eyes while the genie spoke her magic words. When he opened them, the genie was gone. He looked down at himself and saw that he was invisible! It worked!

7 "Omar went outside where some of his friends were playing baseball. He went up to his friend Ralph and asked if he could play. Ralph jumped and looked to see who was talking. The other children got scared and ran away. Omar went to the playground, and the same thing happened.

8 "When Omar returned home, he went upstairs to his bedroom. He had a sad look on his face, but no one could see it. Omar realized that being invisible was not as much fun as he thought it would be. He closed his eyes and began to wish as hard as he could. Once again the genie appeared. 'Please take my wish back!' Omar cried. 'I want people to be able to see me again!'

9 "The genie smiled. 'I see you have learned something today,' said the genie. Then she snapped her fingers and disappeared. Omar looked down and could see himself again. He ran downstairs and cried to his parents. 'You can see me again!'

10 "'Well, I'm glad you're home,' said his mother. 'You're in big trouble for not finishing your chores.' Omar never thought he would be so glad to sweep the floor."

11 Peter looked at his hands and then said, "Maybe being invisible isn't such a good wish after all."

12 Then he sighed. "I guess that means I have to finish my homework."

13 "I guess it does," agreed Mandy.

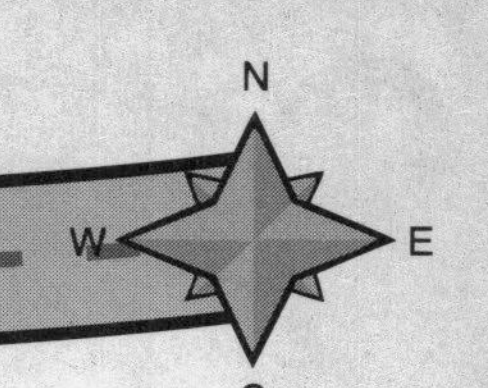

1 **Look at this sentence from the selection.**

> **"Why <u>would</u> that be bad?" asked Peter.**

Which of the words below rhymes with <u>would</u>?

- ○ **A** good
- ○ **B** wool
- ○ **C** dog
- ○ **D** bought

2 **Look at the picture below.**

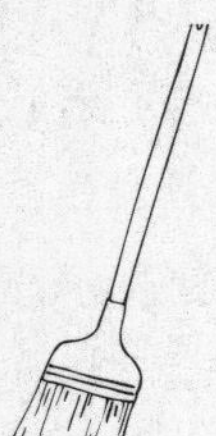

Which word below has the same vowel sound as the word in the picture?

- ○ **F** moan
- ○ **G** bone
- ○ **H** spoon
- ○ **J** crumb

3 **Read this sentence from the selection.**

> **Once again the genie <u>appeared</u>.**

Which word below has the same beginning sound as <u>appeared</u>?

- ○ **A** invisible
- ○ **B** apple
- ○ **C** prepare
- ○ **D** purpose

4 **Read the two sentences below.**

> **The __________ about Omar taught Peter a lesson. Now he will _____ his homework.**

Which pair of words properly completes the sentences above?

- ○ **F** tail, do
- ○ **G** tale, due
- ○ **H** tail, due
- ○ **J** tale, do

5 **Which word from the selection rhymes with the word <u>more</u>?**

- ○ **A** genie
- ○ **B** fun
- ○ **C** once
- ○ **D** floor

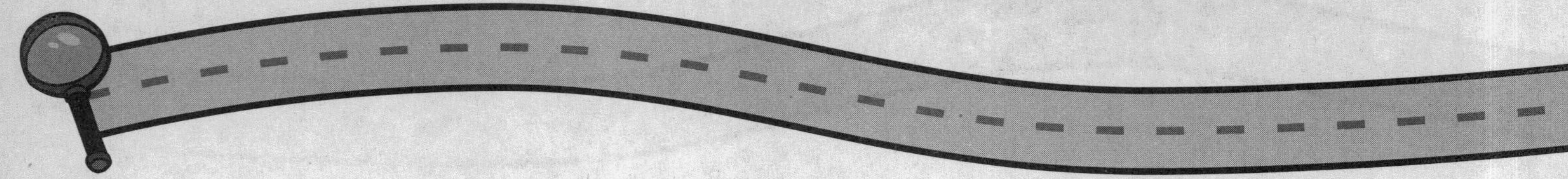

Directions: Read this story about a mean bear and a smart mouse. Then answer the questions that follow.

The Bear and the Mouse

1 There once was a giant bear who lived in the forest. The bear was very strong. He was also very cruel. He was mean to all the other animals in the forest. The other animals were all afraid of the bear.

2 One day a small mouse named Whiskers was drinking at a stream. The bear saw her and pushed Whiskers into the water.

3 "Why did you do that?" asked Whiskers.

4 "This is my stream," said the bear. "If you want to drink here, you must ask my permission first."

5 "May I have some water?" asked Whiskers.

6 "No," yelled the bear, who then laughed. "Now go away before I get mad."

7 Whiskers was very angry. She was too small to fight the bear. But she had one thing that the bear did not have. She had friends. Whiskers gathered together all the animals of the forest. There were mice, raccoons, foxes, deer, and birds.

8 "My friends, we must do something about the mean bear. He is making our lives unhappy," said Whiskers.

9 "But what can we do?" asked an older mouse. "The bear is big, and we are small."

10 "That is true," said Whiskers, "but there is only one bear. There are many of us. If we stand up to him together, he will not be able to hurt us." The other animals listened to Whiskers's plan and agreed with it.

11 The next day Whiskers went back to the stream. Soon the bear saw her and ran to the stream. "I told you that this stream was mine!" said the bear. "I did not say that you could drink here."

12 The bear was surprised when the little mouse did not run away. Whiskers told the bear that the animals were not afraid of him. Then she told the bear to leave her alone.

13 The bear got very angry at Whiskers. But suddenly the bear heard a loud sound. He looked up and saw a sky full of birds. Then he looked around and saw all of the forest animals in the trees. "You can't be mean to us anymore," Whiskers said. "You may be bigger than us, but we will stick together."

14 The bear realized that he could not win against so many other animals. He agreed not to be mean to the animals anymore. That is why the largest animal does not always rule the forest.

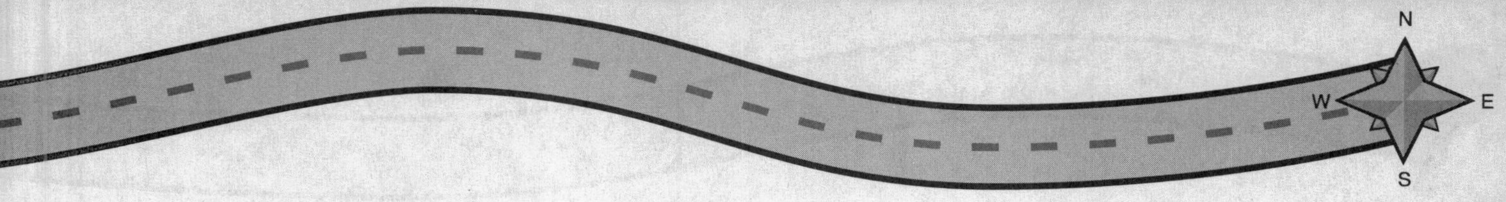

6 **Read this sentence.**

> **Whiskers was tired of the ______ being a bully. She wanted all of the animals to live in ______.**

Which pair of words completes the sentences?

- ○ **F** bare, piece
- ○ **G** bear, peace
- ○ **H** bare, peace
- ○ **J** bear, piece

7 **Look at this sentence.**

> **"The bear is big, and <u>we are</u> small."**

Which answer choice shows a different way of writing <u>we are</u>?

- ○ **A** we're
- ○ **B** we'd
- ○ **C** w're
- ○ **D** were

8 **Which list of words shows that someone is DOING something?**

- ○ **F** you, animals, they, bear
- ○ **G** told, hurt, ran, drink
- ○ **H** forest, edge, here, her
- ○ **J** largest, always, never, back

9 **Look at the picture below.**

Which word has the same vowel sound as the word for what is shown in this picture?

- ○ **A** could
- ○ **B** soon
- ○ **C** bear
- ○ **D** mouse

10 **Read this sentence from the selection.**

> **"No," <u>yelled</u> the bear, who then laughed.**

Which of these words sounds the same in the middle as <u>yelled</u>?

- ○ **F** team
- ○ **G** steel
- ○ **H** jelly
- ○ **J** crease

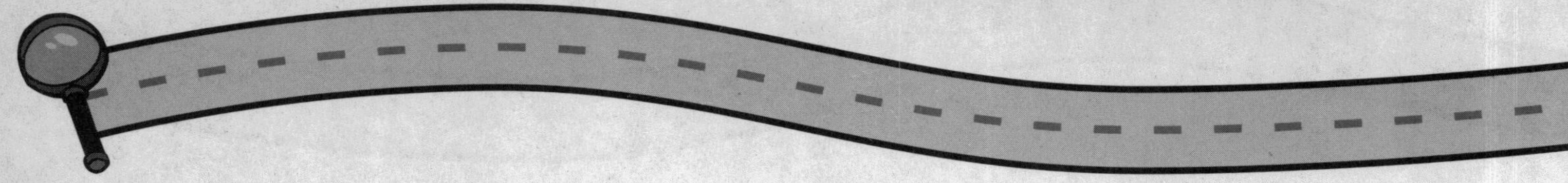

Directions: Read this story about a silly girl named Lila. Then answer the questions that follow.

Lila and Her Coin

1 There once was a young girl who lived in a small town. The girl's name was Lila. Lila was very smart, but sometimes she did not pay attention. Her family said she spent too much time dreaming and not enough time working. Lila would often daydream in school and would miss the entire lesson.

2 One day Lila's parents asked her to buy some fruit for the family at the store in town. Her father gave her a shiny new coin to pay for the fruit. He told her to put the coin in her pocket. But Lila was already thinking about something else. She did not listen to what her father said.

3 On the way into town, Lila thought about all of the wonderful things she could do with her father's coin. Lila thought that maybe her family would prefer to have bread instead of fruit. Or maybe some fresh eggs would be tastier than fruit. Lila also thought about buying a pet for the family. "A new puppy would bring a lot more joy than a bunch of fruit," she thought to herself. "My father would be so proud if I brought home a new dog for us to play with."

4 Lila was so busy thinking about buying a new puppy for the family that she did not see a rock in front of her. She tripped over the rock in the road and fell on her knees. The coin, which she had never put in her pocket, flew out of her hand. It rolled down the road. It rolled all the way into a gutter on the side of the road, and it was gone.

5 Dr. Rollins, a neighbor who saw what happened, came over to help Lila up. "I am sorry about your money," she told Lila. "But don't worry, I'm sure your parents will not be angry."

6 Lila thanked Dr. Rollins for her help. But she knew she had lost the coin because she did not pay attention. "From now on," she said, "I will always pay attention to what people tell me."

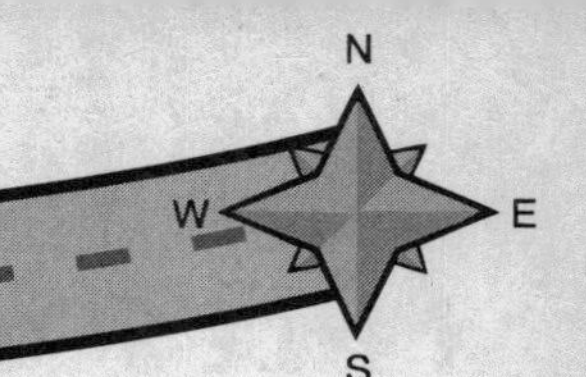

11 Read the sentence from the selection below.

> "But don't worry, I'm sure your parents will not be angry."

Which answer shows a different way to write don't?

- ○ **A** does not
- ○ **B** do not
- ○ **C** did not
- ○ **D** dare not

12 Look at the sentence below from the selection.

> Or maybe some fresh eggs would be tastier than fruit.

Which word below rhymes with the word eggs?

- ○ **F** logs
- ○ **G** sags
- ○ **H** digs
- ○ **J** begs

13 Look at the drawing below.

Which word below has the same ending sound as the word that names what is in this picture?

- ○ **A** coin
- ○ **B** road
- ○ **C** bone
- ○ **D** young

14 Which word below from the selection rhymes with the word keys?

- ○ **F** knees
- ○ **G** one
- ○ **H** rock
- ○ **J** your

15 Read this sentence from the selection.

> Lila would often daydream in school and would miss the entire lesson.

Which word below has the same beginning sound as school?

- ○ **A** shark
- ○ **B** chore
- ○ **C** skate
- ○ **D** check

MILE 10: BEFORE READING STORIES

You can learn a lot about a reading passage even before you've read its first sentence. For example, the title of a book often will give you a hint as to whether it's a made-up story or it's about interesting facts. Think about the title *Discovering Turtles.* Just from the title alone, you know that this book will tell you interesting facts about turtles.

Directions: Look at the book covers on the next two pages. On the lines below each cover, write what you think the book is about. Use the titles and the art on the covers to help you decide what the books are about.

1

____

____

2

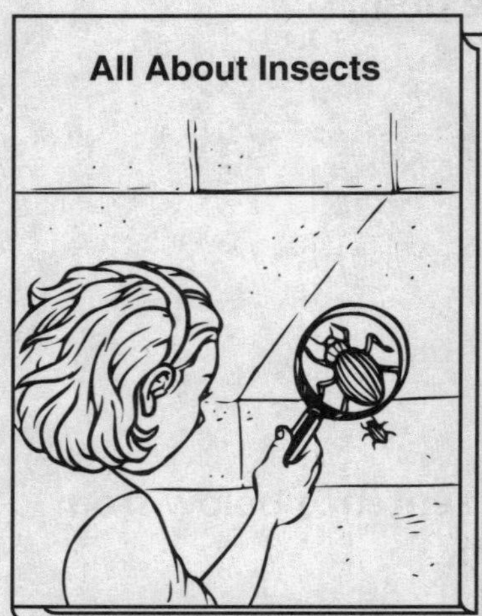

____

____

3

____

____

4

____

____

5

6

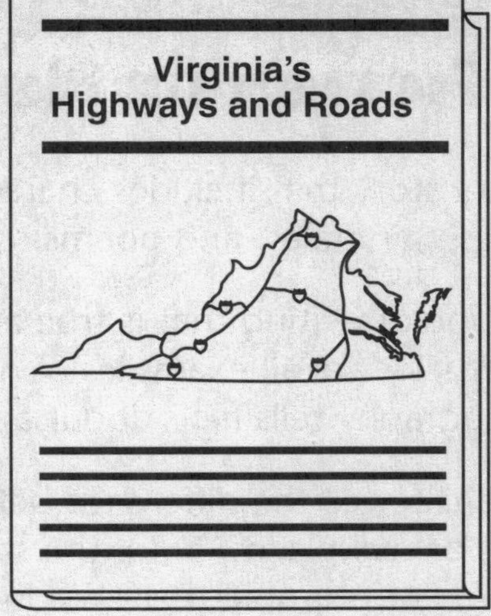

7

8

See—sometimes you *can* judge a book by its cover!

Mile 11: Fiction or Nonfiction?

Fiction is a type of story that includes characters and events that are imagined. Fiction can include stories, fairy tales, and poems.

Nonfiction is a type of writing that is true and contains facts. Instructions, textbooks, and newspaper articles are all examples of nonfiction writing. Nonfiction provides information. A biography tells facts about a real person. That means it is nonfiction.

Sometimes it's hard to tell the difference between fiction and nonfiction. Some stories contain true facts or real places. But if the story includes any imagined characters or events, it is fiction. For example there is a famous folktale about Paul Bunyon. A story about a giant man who could chop down mountains can't be true. But the story about him happened in real places, such as the Great Plains. Because Paul Bunyon didn't really exist, the story is fiction.

A tall tale is also an example of fiction. Stories about talking animals or giant people may be called tall tales. Tall tales aren't true.

Directions: Below are two book titles. One is fiction, and one is nonfiction. Write "Fiction" below the fiction book. Write "Nonfiction" below the nonfiction book.

A

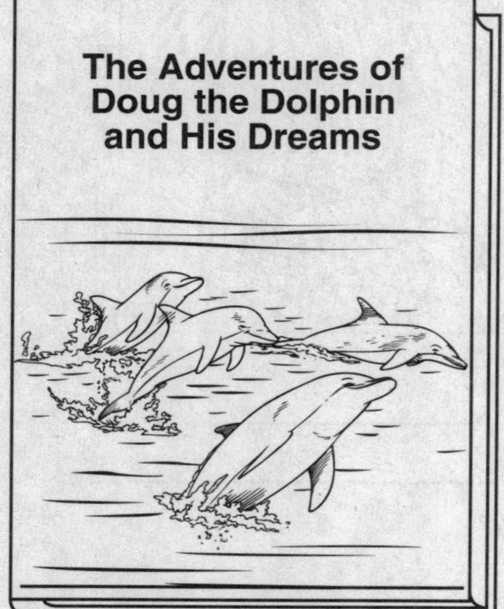

____

B

____

Directions: Below are sentences taken from ***The Adventures of Doug the Dolphin and His Dreams*** and ***Facts About Dolphins.*** Decide which book the sentences come from. Read each sentence. Then write either "fiction" or "nonfiction" on the line next to it.

1 Dolphins are among the smartest animals in the world. ____________

2 Doug leaped out of the water, laughing all the while. ____________

3 The dolphin was sad when he learned that his best friend was missing. ____________

4 Scientists believe that dolphins are distantly related to cows. ____________

5 A dolphin has a powerful tail that allows it to swim very fast. ____________

6 Doug's mother spent part of each day teaching him how to catch fish. ____________

7 Dolphins are mammals. They have hair and use lungs to breathe air. ____________

8 The dolphins gathered every night to tell stories. ____________

9 Sally the Dolphin decided that they would look for the hidden treasure together. ____________

10 All dolphins use sounds to locate objects in the water. ____________

11 Dolphins are found in oceans all over the world. ____________

12 The dolphin's greatest wish was to travel all the way around the world. ____________

13 The dolphins watched as the boat containing their friends sailed away. ____________

14 Dolphins have been known to rescue sailors stranded in the ocean. ____________

15 Many people think that dolphins can talk to each ____________

On the lines below write one fiction sentence and one nonfiction sentence that you think could be in each book. Use the sentences above as models.

Fiction:

____

Nonfiction:

____

MILE 12: WHY DO PEOPLE READ?

People read for many different reasons. There are probably three major reasons that people read.

- People read to have fun.
- People read to gain knowledge.
- People read to learn how to do things.

Directions: Look at the different types of subjects below. Each example shows a different type of writing. On the next page are the three different reasons people read. Write the name of each kind of reading selection under the column that best describes why someone would read it. Cross out the book after you have written your answer. You should do this to make sure you don't write the same book twice. The first example has been done for you.

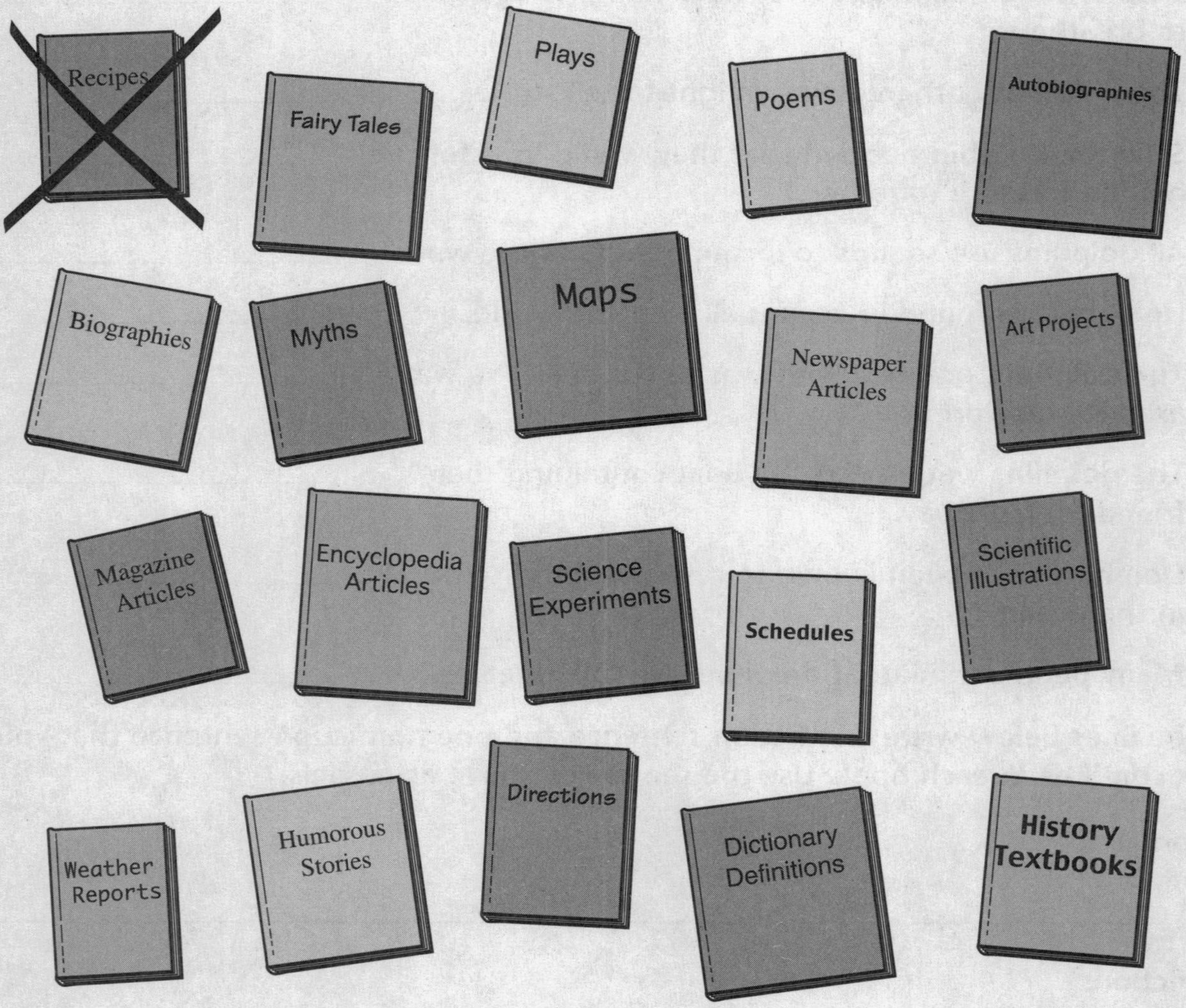

Recipes
Fairy Tales
Plays
Poems
Autobiographies
Biographies
Myths
Maps
Newspaper Articles
Art Projects
Magazine Articles
Encyclopedia Articles
Science Experiments
Schedules
Scientific Illustrations
Weather Reports
Humorous Stories
Directions
Dictionary Definitions
History Textbooks

Keep in mind that the answers aren't set in stone. For example, people read newspapers to gain information, but they also may read them to have fun.

To have fun	To gain knowledge	To learn how to do things
		Recipes

Directions: The words in the box below list six different types of reading selections. Read each of the short selections on this page and the next one. Use the words from the box to complete the sentence that follows each selection. Then answer the questions. You may use each word listed in the box more than once. The first one has been done for you.

a poem	an encyclopedia article	a story
a recipe	a biography	a dictionary

1 **Broom. *n.* An object used to sweep the floor.**

This reading selection is from a dictionary.

Why might somebody read this selection? Somebody might read this selection to find out the meaning of a word.

2 **Add 3 cups of sugar. Stir quickly. Pour mixture into the hot water.**

This reading selection is from ________________.

Why might somebody read this selection? ________________

____

3 **The moose is a large mammal of the northern United States and Canada. The males have wide, flat antlers on their heads.**

This reading selection is from ________________.

Why might somebody read this selection? ________________

____

4 **Tomas and Maria watched the rocket take off. They were excited about their first trip to the space station.**

This reading selection is from ________________.

Why might somebody read this selection? ________________

____

5 **George Washington was the first president of the United States. Even before that, he had a long and exciting life.**

This reading selection is from ________________.

Why might somebody read this selection? ________________

____

6 Apples and elms, oaks so high.
Maples and firs, towering to the sky.

This reading selection is from ____.

Why might somebody read this selection? ______________________________

____

7 Remove the cake from the oven using pot holders. Then let the cake cool for 10 minutes.

This reading selection is from ____.

Why might somebody read this selection? ______________________________

____

8 The bear and the fox agreed that the wolf had been stealing their food.

This reading selection is from ____.

Why might somebody read this selection? ______________________________

____

9 Cat. *n.* A small animal often kept as a pet.

This reading selection is from ____.

Why might somebody read this selection? ______________________________

____

10 Swimming with the happy fish,
The pond fulfills my every wish.

This reading selection is from ____.

Why might somebody read this selection? ______________________________

____

11 Babe Ruth was born as George Herman Ruth. He was one of the most popular baseball players in the history of the sport.

This reading selection is from ____.

Why might somebody read this selection? ______________________________

____

Mile 13: Finding the Main Idea

The **main idea** of a reading selection is what the selection is mostly about. A longer reading selection can have more than one main idea. When you write a **summary,** you put the main ideas of the reading selection in your own words.

Directions: Below you will find four short passages. Read each one and then answer the questions that follow. The first one has been done for you.

Mike and Jane were playing on the swings. Suddenly Jane saw something moving in the grass below. It was a snake! Mike saw it, too, and he began to yell. Jane jumped off her swing and looked at the snake. She saw that it was a harmless grass snake. Mike yelled at her not to touch it, but she picked it up anyway. She told Mike not to be afraid. Jane said that her mother worked at the zoo and had taught her about this kind of snake. Mike slowly reached out and touched the snake. He was surprised by how cool and smooth it felt. It wasn't so bad after all!

1 **What would be a good title for this passage?**

Jane Finds a Snake

2 **What is the main idea of this passage?** *Mike learns not to be afraid of snakes.*

Snakes, lizards, turtles, and crocodiles are all reptiles. Reptiles have scales on their bodies. The scales are hard and help to protect the animals. They help prevent scratches and cuts. It is like wearing a suit of armor. The scales of a reptile grow inside the skin. A turtle shell is special. It is made out of bone, and the scales grow over it. As a reptile grows, it sheds the skin that covers the scales. In most reptiles, the skin comes off in pieces. However, snakes often shed their skins in one long piece.

3 **What would be a good title for this passage?**

____

4 **What is the main idea of this passage?** ______________________________

____

The people in the town had all heard about the stranger who had arrived the night before. No one knew her name. Someone said that the stranger dressed all in black. Many people thought that she was a criminal. Some folks even said they should call the sheriff. Finally they decided to find out who she was. The toughest people in town walked to her house. They pounded on the door and demanded to see her. When the stranger opened the door, they asked her who she was. She smiled and told them, "I'm the new pastor. You can find me every day at the church!"

5 What would be a good title for this passage?

____

6 What is the main idea of this passage? ______________________

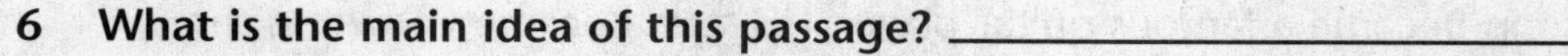

____

Have you ever wondered why cowboys dress the way they do? Each piece of clothing serves a purpose. The big hats they wear help protect cowboys from sun and rain. The pieces of leather they wear over their pants protect them from thorns, rocks, and insect bites. The pointed toes and big heels of their boots help keep their feet in the stirrups when they ride horses. Even the handkerchiefs some cowboys wear over their faces have a purpose. It doesn't mean they are bank robbers, either! The handkerchief helps keep dust out of their noses and mouths when they are riding.

7 What would be a good title for this passage?

____

8 What is the main idea of this passage? ______________________

____

You need to answer the questions on the test based on what you've read in the passages. Do not answer the questions based on what you might already know about a topic.

Directions: Read the following passage and think about the main idea. On the next page, do the writing activities about this passage.

Chet Atkins

1 Chet Atkins was born in Tennessee in 1924. He began playing the guitar at a young age. By the time he was 22 years old, he was playing in bands. As time went by, he developed a special style. His finger-picking technique sounded like classical and country music combined. When he was 23 years old, he got his first recording contract. His first record album, *Chet Atkins' Galloping Guitar,* was released in 1954. It contained his first hit, "Mr. Sandman."

2 Atkins soon became a famous guitar player. His style became known as the Nashville sound, because that's where he started playing. Atkins did not just write and record songs. He produced records for many famous musicians. He produced Elvis Presley's first hits. Atkins was also a member of Presley's first band.

3 Atkins became the president of RCA Records in Nashville. There he produced records for other famous country and western musicians. He also played guitar on many of their records. Atkins worked for RCA until 1981. During this time he produced many hit records. He often wrote songs for other artists that became big hits. He continued to record his own music as well.

4 Atkins was a role model for many guitar players. In 1973 he became a member of the Country Music Hall of Fame. He won lots of awards, including 13 Grammys. He recorded more than 120 albums in his life. Atkins continued to make music until June 2001. He died at the age of 77.

9 **Write a short summary of this passage about Chet Atkins. Your summary should include only the most important ideas about Atkins.**

10 **Write down the main idea of the entire passage on the lines below.**

Map Check 3

Directions: Read the following passage and then answer the questions that follow.

Stella's New Friend

1 Stella lay on her back and watched the clouds float by overhead. Beneath her the dock slowly rocked in time with the waves. Stella sighed and yawned. As she lay there, a voice beneath her asked, "Little human girl, what is the matter?" Stella jumped to her feet and looked all around.

2 "Who said that?" she cried. She looked everywhere, but could not see a single person.

3 "I did," said the voice. "Look under the dock." Stella bent over and looked under the wooden pier. There in the water was a beautiful dolphin. As Stella watched, the dolphin waved a flipper and squeaked happily. "Hello!" said the dolphin. "My name is Morris."

4 "A talking dolphin!" said Stella with a grin. "I never knew dolphins could talk."

5 "Oh, yes, we can talk. We are just careful who we talk to. What are you doing up there?"

6 "Nothing," said Stella. "That is the problem. I have nothing to do."

7 "I know something we can do," said Morris. "We can play games and have fun! Dolphins always know the best games."

8 "All right," said Stella. "But I cannot go into the water when there are no adults around," she told Morris.

9 "That is fine," said Morris. "Do you have a ball? We could play catch." Stella ran back to her house and found a ball. She went to the beach and stood by the edge of the water.

10 "Over here!" she called to Morris. Morris leaped into the air and right over the dock. He made a huge splash when he came down.

11 "Whee!" he yelled. He swam over to where Stella was standing. "Throw me the ball," he told her. Stella threw the ball into the water. Instead of catching it, Morris bumped it with his head. It sailed through the air right back to Stella. She threw it again, and this time Morris smacked it with his tail. Once again, it went right into Stella's hands. Stella laughed and clapped her hands. Morris laughed and slapped his flippers on the water.

12 For the next hour they played catch. When Stella's mother called her in for dinner, she did not want to leave. "Go ahead," said Morris. "We will play again tomorrow. I will come back the same time as today."

13 With that, he dove into the water and swam away. Stella could not believe her good luck. She wondered how she would ever get to sleep that night because she was so excited about her new friend.

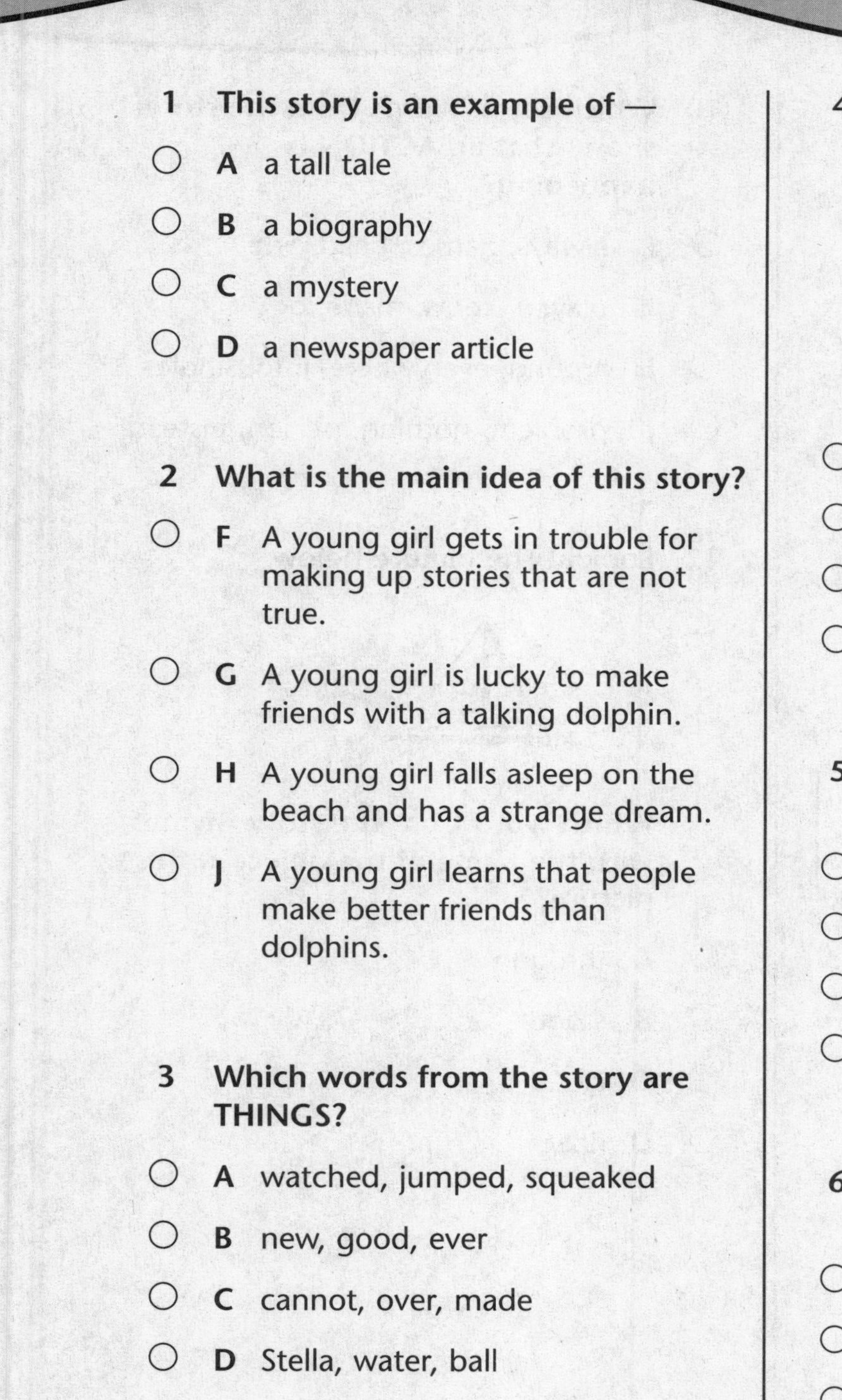

1 This story is an example of —

- ○ **A** a tall tale
- ○ **B** a biography
- ○ **C** a mystery
- ○ **D** a newspaper article

2 What is the main idea of this story?

- ○ **F** A young girl gets in trouble for making up stories that are not true.
- ○ **G** A young girl is lucky to make friends with a talking dolphin.
- ○ **H** A young girl falls asleep on the beach and has a strange dream.
- ○ **J** A young girl learns that people make better friends than dolphins.

3 Which words from the story are THINGS?

- ○ **A** watched, jumped, squeaked
- ○ **B** new, good, ever
- ○ **C** cannot, over, made
- ○ **D** Stella, water, ball

4 Read the two sentences below about the story.

Morris liked it when Stella _________ the ball to him. He would play catch for _______.

Which pair of words completes the sentences the right way?

- ○ **F** through, hours
- ○ **G** threw, hours
- ○ **H** threw, ours
- ○ **J** through, ours

5 Which word from the story rhymes with <u>teach</u>?

- ○ **A** catch
- ○ **B** right
- ○ **C** dock
- ○ **D** beach

6 Which words from the story DESCRIBE other words?

- ○ **F** sailed, where, laughed, cannot
- ○ **G** doing, beach, water, throw
- ○ **H** good, new, huge, beautiful
- ○ **J** smacked, tail, dove, wondered

7 **Which answer choice BEST describes the lesson that Stella learns in this story?**

○ **A** Stella learns that dolphins get people in trouble.

○ **B** Stella learns how to swim in the ocean.

○ **C** Stella learns that the beach is a boring place.

○ **D** Stella learns that it is exciting to make new friends.

8 **Read the following sentence from the story.**

> **Stella could not believe her good luck.**

Which of the answer choices below shows the correct way to join could and not?

○ **F** couldn't

○ **G** can't

○ **H** shouldn't

○ **J** didn't

9 **Which word from the story has the same vowel sound as bend?**

○ **A** sleep

○ **B** here

○ **C** made

○ **D** friend

10 **Which set of words from the story shows that an ACTION is happening?**

○ **F** always, games, head, fine

○ **G** played, know, made, go

○ **H** around, everywhere, into, single

○ **J** problem, nothing, person, instead

11 **Look at the picture below.**

Which word from the story rhymes with the name of the object in this picture?

○ **A** through

○ **B** stood

○ **C** cloud

○ **D** float

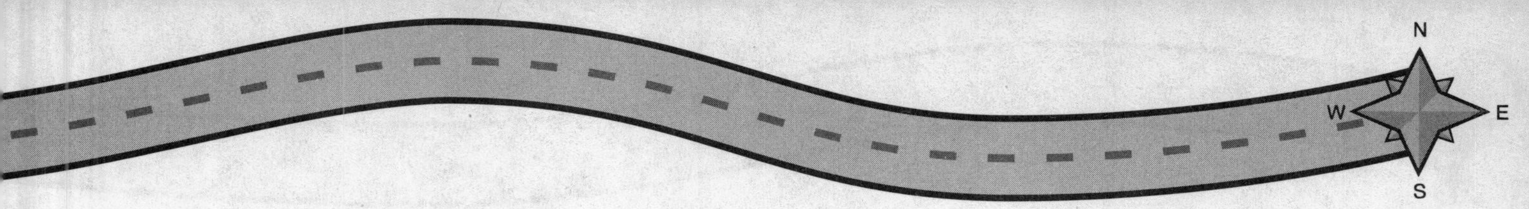

Directions: Read the selection and then answer the questions that follow.

The Wolf and the Fox

1 Many, many years ago a wolf and a fox were walking through the woods. They were hungry and looking for food. Suddenly the wolf smelled something in the air. "Do you smell that?" the wolf asked the fox.

2 "Yes," said the fox. "It smells like food. Let us see where the smell is coming from." Together the two friends crept through the bushes. When they reached a clearing, they peeked between the branches. To their surprise, they saw a small group of people standing by a fire. The people were cooking food.

3 The wolf and the fox had seen people before, but never this close. They watched the people cooking the food over the fire. The wolf saw that the people had several large fish. They also had fruits and vegetables that they had found in the forest.

4 The fox watched until his stomach started to make noise. "We have got to get some of that food," said the fox. "I am so hungry that my belly hurts."

5 "Mine too," said the wolf. "But how can we get the food? The people look very strong."

6 "I have heard that if you make a lot of noise and show your teeth, people will run away," the fox told the wolf.

7 "Where did you hear that?" asked the wolf. "I have heard that people are very brave."

8 "My friend the bear told me," said the fox. "Now I am going to scare the people away from the food." With that, the fox jumped out of the bushes and went running straight at the people. He growled and showed his teeth. The people, seeing the small fox running at them, began to laugh. They picked up stones and threw them at the fox until he turned around and ran away. The fox ran back into the bushes where the wolf was hiding. "I don't understand," he said. "I did just what the bear told me."

9 "Perhaps it is because the bear is larger than the largest person, and you are smaller than the smallest child. I think I will try something different." The wolf began walking toward the people. He kept his head down and put a sad look on his face. When the people saw him, they felt sorry for the wolf and tossed some food to him. From then on the wolf became friends with the people and helped protect them from danger. And the fox stayed in the woods, away from people.

12 **What kind of story is this?**

○ F a true story

○ G a biography

● H a fable

○ J a poem

13 **Which words from the story show that an ACTION is happening?**

○ A many, wild, like, suddenly

● B watched, crept, walking, picked

○ C clearing, food, over, some

○ D strong, very, back, around

14 **Read the following sentence from the story.**

> **"I <u>don't</u> understand," he said.**

Which of the answers below shows another way to write <u>don't</u>?

○ F did not

○ G is not

○ H could not

● J do not

15 **Which of the words below rhymes with the word <u>fox</u>?**

○ A lock

● B rocks

○ C brick

○ D junk

16 **What is the main idea of this story?**

● F Two animals learn an important lesson.

○ G A wolf learns that it is not as smart as a fox.

○ H People learn to be scared of all wild animals.

○ J The fox learns that he is braver than the wolf.

17 **Which of the words below has the same beginning sound as <u>smell</u>?**

○ A think

○ B choose

○ C shower

● D smile

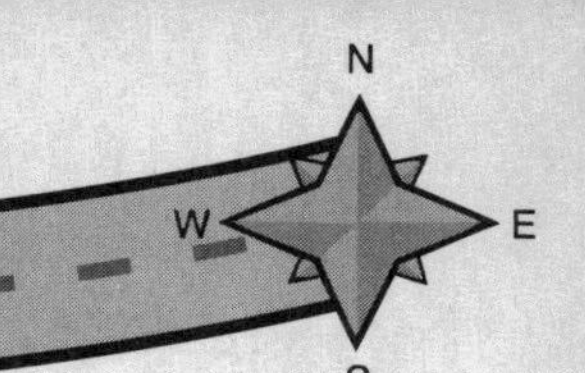

18 **Read this sentence.**

> **The fox thought he had learned something ________ about people from the ________.**

Which pair of words below correctly completes the sentence?

- F knew, bare
- G new, bare
- H knew, bear
- J new, bear

19 **Which sentence BEST describes the lesson of this story?**

- A A wolf learns that being nice is important.
- B A wolf learns to listen to the fox.
- C People think that the fox is funny.
- D A bear learns that it can scare people.

20 **Look at this picture.**

What word from the story has the same middle and end sounds as what is shown in the picture?

- F wolf
- G fire
- H bear
- J bushes

21 **Look at this sentence from the story.**

> **He kept his head down and put a sad look on his face.**

Which word below rhymes with down?

- A frown
- B lean
- C drain
- D plow

22 **Read the two sentences below.**

> **The fox watched until his stomach started to make noise. "We have got to get some of that food," said the fox.**

What choice below shows a different way to say we have got like it was used in the sentence above?

- F we're got
- G we've got
- H we'll got
- J we'd got

Mile 14: Finding Supporting Ideas

Supporting ideas are facts that tell more about the main idea. For example, a selection about the lives of bees might tell how bees are born, how they make honey, and why they might sting you. These facts about the lives of bees are the supporting ideas.

Directions: Read the passage about wolves below and then do the activity on the next page.

1 Wolves have been around for thousands of years. However, scientists are still learning new things about these beautiful animals.

2 Wolves live across the northern hemisphere of the world. There are two basic types of wolves. The gray wolf lives in Canada, the northern United States, Alaska, northern Europe, and Russia. It is also called the timber wolf. The second type of wolf is the red wolf. It lives only in the southeastern United States and Texas.

3 Although most gray wolves are gray, they can also have many other colors of fur. Some are red, yellow, or black. Many have patches of brown, white, gray, or black on top of another color. In the far north, some gray wolves are actually pure white.

4 Gray wolves also come in many sizes. Some can be smaller than a large dog such as a German shepherd. Others may weigh as much as 175 pounds. The red wolf is smaller than the gray wolf.

5 Wolves live in groups called packs. Each pack has two leaders. A male and a female wolf run a pack together. Some packs are small and contain only five or six wolves. Other packs are larger and contain as many as fifteen wolves. The size of the pack depends on many things. The most important is food. When a lot of food is available, wolves will live in larger packs. When food is hard to find, a large pack will split into smaller packs. Wolves hunt for food together and they share what they catch. The pack leaders and babies get to eat first. The rest of the pack eats what is left over.

6 Wolves are very smart and can "talk" to each other in special ways. Lifting a tail or ear a certain way means something to other wolves such as "let's play," or "leave me alone." Wolves often howl. This sound can mean that it is time to gather and hunt. It can also be a way of telling other wolves "this is my land, stay away." Sometimes wolves howl just because they are happy.

7 Wolves have a very good sense of smell and can "see" much better with their noses than people can with their eyes. A wolf can tell if an animal is sick or angry. It can smell how far away water is. A wolf can even tell what the weather will be just by the way the air smells!

The main idea of the passage you have just read is written in the center of the graphic organizer below. Write the supporting ideas in the spaces provided. The first one has been done for you.

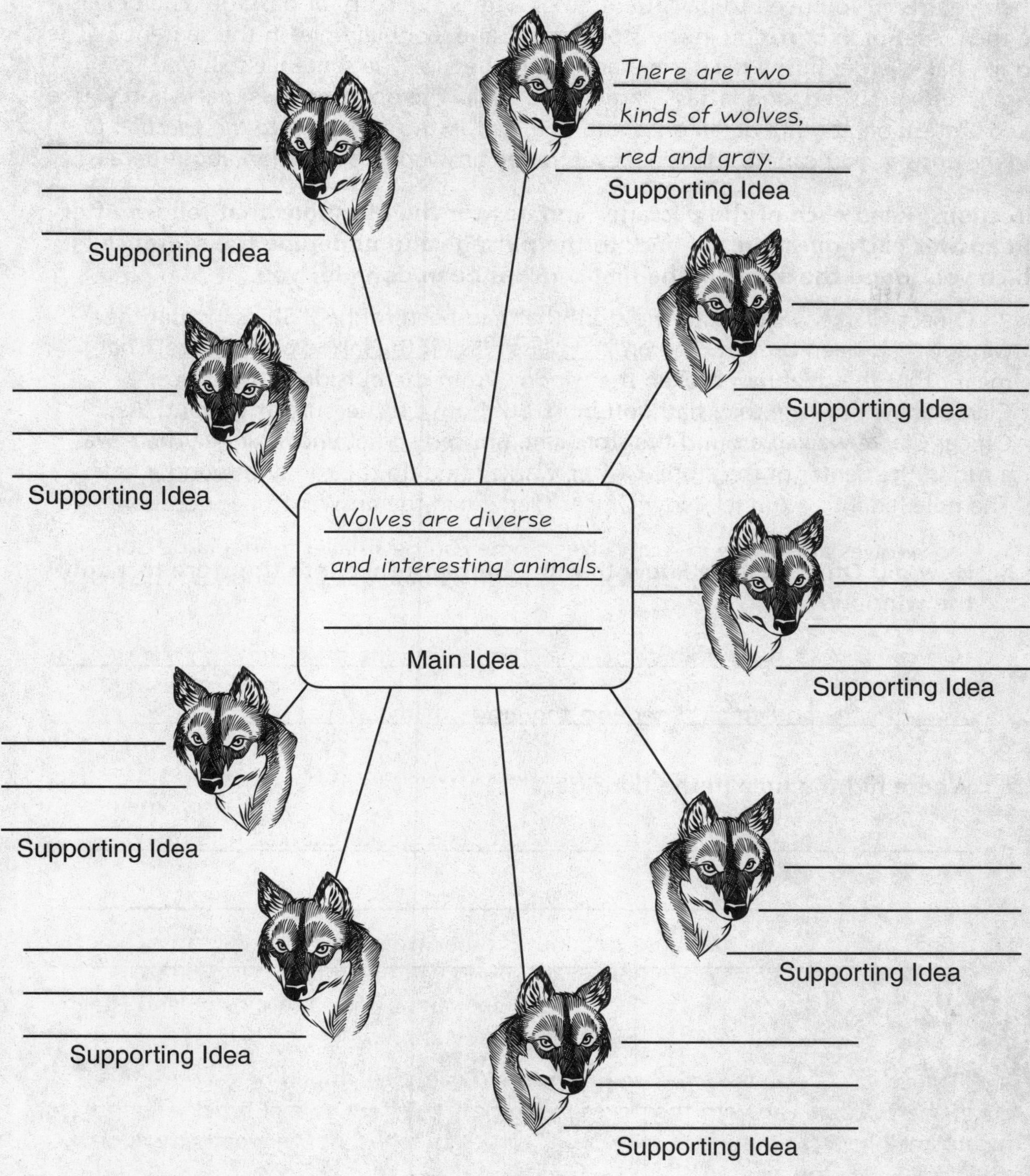

MILE 15: ANSWERING QUESTIONS ABOUT DETAILS

When you read, you need to pay attention to details in a story or passage. The details are the pieces of information in the story or passage. For example, in the sentence "The red fox has a large, bushy tail," there are several details. The sentence tells you that there is a fox, it is red, and it has a large, bushy tail. The good news is that when you're asked a question about a detail on a test, you can *always refer back to the selection to find the answer*. You can do this whenever you're answering a question about details.

Directions: Read each of the passages and answer the questions that follow. After you answer each question, go back to the passage and underline the sentence in which you found the answer. The first one has been done for you.

Officer Clarke walked into the store that had been robbed. She saw that the window had been broken. <u>The broken glass was on the inside of the store.</u> That meant that the thief had broken the window from the outside. Now Officer Clarke knew how the thief had gotten in. But how did the burglar get out? As Officer Clarke walked around the store, she noticed something strange. There was a rug in the center of the store. Officer Clarke lifted up the rug and found a hole. The hole led into a tunnel. Now Officer Clarke had the answer to her question.

1 **How did Officer Clarke know that the burglar broke into the store through the window?**

Officer Clarke knew that the burglar broke into the store through the window because the broken glass was on the inside of the store.

2 **Where did the hole in the floor go?**

____

____

____

The job of a real-life detective is very different from what you see on television. Detectives spend a lot of their time looking for clues. Even more time is spent trying to piece them together. Solving a crime is like putting a puzzle together when you do not have all the pieces. A detective must be very patient. The tiniest clue could solve a mystery. A piece of hair or thread could be the last piece of a puzzle. A real detective spends more time looking for clues than chasing criminals.

3 According to the author, what is solving a crime like?

____

4 Real detectives spend more time looking for clues than doing what?

____

The bubbles cleared away from his face as his feet touched the bottom. When he reached the bottom, he turned on his flashlight. The diver looked around and saw the sunken ship a few feet away. He walked slowly to the wreck, his heavy boots keeping him from floating. The only sound the diver could hear was his own breath. It was time to start looking for the treasure!

5 What is the diver looking for?

____

6 Why doesn't the diver float while he is in the water?

____

Today, scuba divers carry their air with them in special tanks on their backs. However, diving used to be very different. Early divers wore special suits with heavy metal helmets. Hoses from a ship connected to the helmet. These hoses carried air for the diver. Divers wore heavy weights on their chests to keep them from floating. Some diving suits weighed more than 250 pounds. A diver had to be very strong to walk in one. These divers faced many dangers. Air hoses could get caught on rocks. Sometimes the helmets or suits leaked. Many early divers did not live past the age of 30.

7 According to this passage, what was one of the dangers early divers faced?

____

8 Where do divers carry their air today?

____

MILE 16: LEARNING NEW WORDS

You often will see a word that you do not know the meaning of. You can often figure out what the word means from the sentences around it. Look at the example below.

> "The man placed the nail against the wall and **walloped** it with his hammer. When the hammer hit the nail, there was a loud bang."

You may not know what the word **wallop** means, but the second sentence gives you a clue. It says that the hammer *hit* the nail. If you replace *wallop* with *hit,* the sentence makes sense. Now you know that *hit* and *wallop* mean the same thing.

Directions: Sometimes a person can learn an important lesson in the most unusual way. Read this passage and see how a tiny ant taught a man a big lesson.

Working Together

1 A long time ago a man was in the forest looking for something to eat. He was having trouble finding food because it had not rained for many days and the plants were **wilting**. He was tired and decided to rest. As he sat on a rock, he looked down and saw a line of ants walking past him. Each ant carried a small piece of food. The man picked up one of the ants and asked it what it was doing.

2 "Why, I am bringing food back to our nest, of course," replied the ant.

3 "Why are you doing that?" asked the man. "Why don't you just eat it? Aren't you hungry?"

4 "Yes, I am **starving,**" said the ant, "but ants all bring their food back to the nest, where we share what we have found."

5 "Why would you do that?" asked the man. "What if you find a big piece of food and another ant does not find anything? Why should that ant get to eat your food?"

6 "Because if we all eat, we are all stronger. That means we can all help protect the nest and look for more food. Besides, what if I am the one who doesn't find any food? By working together our **colony** becomes stronger."

7 "I have never heard of such a thing," said the man. "In my tribe we each eat what we find. We only share with the children who are too small to look for their own food."

8 The ant laughed at this. "That is so strange! Ants would never act like that. And we are not the only ones. The bees also work together as a group. They all gather pollen and use it to make honey. Then, when there is no food to find, they can all share the honey. This is how they stay alive during the winter when there are no flowers to eat. We ants also **store** food for the winter. We gather extra food in the summer and put it into special rooms in our nest. This way, ants never go hungry in the winter."

9 The man thought about this. He remembered many winters when food was **scarce** and he had been very hungry. He said goodbye to the ant and went back to his tribe. He told the members of his tribe that if they all worked together, they could make sure no one went hungry. He said that they should gather extra food now and save it for the winter. The tribe did what the man said and soon became the strongest tribe in the land. Eventually, other tribes saw how the people of the man's tribe helped each other and they began to do the same thing. That is how a single ant changed the way that people lived.

Under each sentence there are three words. Circle the word that means the same thing as the word in bold. You may go back to the passage to find more clues.

1 "He was having trouble finding food because it had not rained for many days and the plants were **wilting.**"

healthy angry weak

2 "Yes, I am **starving,**" said the ant, "but ants all bring their food back to the nest, where we share what we have found."

tired hungry lost

3 "By working together our **colony** becomes stronger."

group friend food

4 "We ants also **store** food for the winter."

spill save buy

5 He remembered many winters when food was **scarce** and he had been very hungry.

everywhere cold rare

MILE 17: DRAWING CONCLUSIONS

Drawing conclusions is easy. You just need to figure out something about a character or a selection based on what you read. Look at the examples below.

"Sally smelled the bottle of perfume and frowned."

Conclusion: Sally does not like the smell of the perfume.

"David munched on his slice of pizza with a look of bliss in his eyes and a giant smile on his face."

Conclusion: David is enjoying his pizza.

Directions: Look at the drawings on the next two pages. Use them to answer the questions that go with each drawing.

1

1 Based on picture 1, why do you think this girl is not going to school?

____

____

____

____

2

2 Based on picture 2, why do you think these people are having a party at this boy's house?

____

____

____

____

3

3 Based on picture 3, why do you think these softball players are celebrating?

4

4 Based on picture 4, why do you think these people are packing their bags?

5

5 Based on picture 5, what do you think this girl and her grandfather are getting ready to do?

Directions: Read the following passage. Notice that some of the sentences are underlined. After you read the passage, answer the questions about the underlined sentences.

1 Benny the Beagle walked down the trail, sniffing the ground as he walked. Benny liked walking through the woods. There were so many good smells to explore. Benny's tail wagged as he walked. He smelled flowers and rabbits and all sorts of things that made him happy to have such a fine nose.

2 Benny walked along with his eyes on the ground. That is why he did not notice the bear on the trail until he walked into him. He shook his head and looked up. When he saw the bear, Benny began to shake. The bear was so big!

3 "Please, Mister Bear, do not hurt me," said Benny. He began to back up slowly, hoping he could run away from the bear.

4 "Don't be afraid," said the bear. "I won't hurt you. My name is Fluffy."

5 Benny looked up at Fluffy and forgot to be scared. "Fluffy? What kind of name is that for a bear?" Benny asked.

6 "When I was a little cub I had big, fluffy hair. That is why my parents named me Fluffy. All my life the other bears have made fun of me. None of them will be my friend, and I cannot make friends with any other animals in the forest. They all think I am going to eat them. They do not believe that I only eat berries, honey, and fish."

7 Benny sat down next to Fluffy. "Well, most animals are much smaller than you. I can understand why they would be afraid of you."

8 "Then why aren't you afraid?" asked Fluffy.

9 "Because I can smell that you are telling the truth," said Benny. "Beagles have very good noses. We can tell when someone is lying, or sick, or angry. Beagles have the best noses around."

10 This amazed Fluffy. His nose was good enough to find honey and berries, but Benny's nose was much better than that. "That gives me an idea," said Fluffy. "You could help me make friends with other animals. You could tell them that I am not dangerous."

11 Benny did not think that other animals would believe him. Every animal he knew was afraid of bears. The other animals might even stop being friends with him if they saw him with a bear. He was going to tell Fluffy he could not help. Then he saw a tear in Fluffy's eye. Benny tried to imagine what it was like to have no friends. Benny knew what he had to do.

12 "All right, I will help you," said Benny. "Just try to look friendly and harmless."

13 Fluffy jumped up in the air and clapped his hands. "Thank you so much! I want to have many friends, but you will always be my first and best friend."

Directions: Think about the story you just read. Answer the questions below, which ask you to draw conclusions. When you draw a conclusion, there must be facts in the story to back it up.

6 Benny's tail wagged as he walked. Why do you think Benny's tail was wagging?

____

____

7 When he saw the bear, Benny began to shake. What do you think is the reason Benny began to shake when he saw the bear?

____

____

8 The other animals might even stop being friends with him if they saw him with a bear. Why would the other animals not want to be Benny's friend if they saw him with Fluffy?

____

____

9 Then he saw a tear in Fluffy's eye. Why do you think Fluffy was crying?

____

Map Check 4

Directions: Read the selection and then answer the questions that follow.

Fulfilling a Dream

Growing Up

1 Carl Brashear was born in 1931. His family was poor. They lived in a time when African American people could not get high-paying jobs. Carl's father worked on a farm. Although Carl was a good student, he had to leave school after the eighth grade to help his father work.

2 Carl always loved the water. His dream was to be a diver for the navy. When he was seventeen years old, he left the farm and enlisted in the navy. He wanted to join the navy diving school, but he was not allowed. The navy said that African Americans could not be divers. Carl ended up working in the kitchen for several years. Finally, an officer let him sign up for diving school.

Carl Loses His Dream

3 Carl was the first African American in the navy diving school. However, because he left school early, he could not pass any of the tests. In 1960 Carl failed diving school. Most people would have given up after that, but Carl did not.

Carl Goes Back to School

4 Carl spent the next two years studying as hard as he could. In 1963 he signed up for diving school a second time. This time he earned one of the best grades in his class. Carl was now a diver.

Carl Loses His Leg

5 Carl Brashear became the first African American navy diver. Many of the other divers did not like this. At first, they made his life very hard, but Carl did not give up. His bravery and skill soon made him one of the best divers in the navy. In 1966 Carl was hurt when a big wave hit his ship. A piece of metal hit Carl in the leg. His leg was hurt so badly that doctors had to cut it off. It seemed that Carl would never dive again.

Carl Doesn't Give Up

6 The navy told Carl that a man with one leg could not be a diver. Carl did not listen. Doctors made a special leg for him to wear. He taught himself how to walk on it. It took many months for him to be able to use the new leg. Carl then convinced the navy that he could dive again. He became the first person to dive with only one real leg. Carl became a top navy diver in 1970.

7 Carl Brashear proved that by working hard and not giving up, a person can overcome almost anything. He once said, "Never let anybody come between you and your dream."

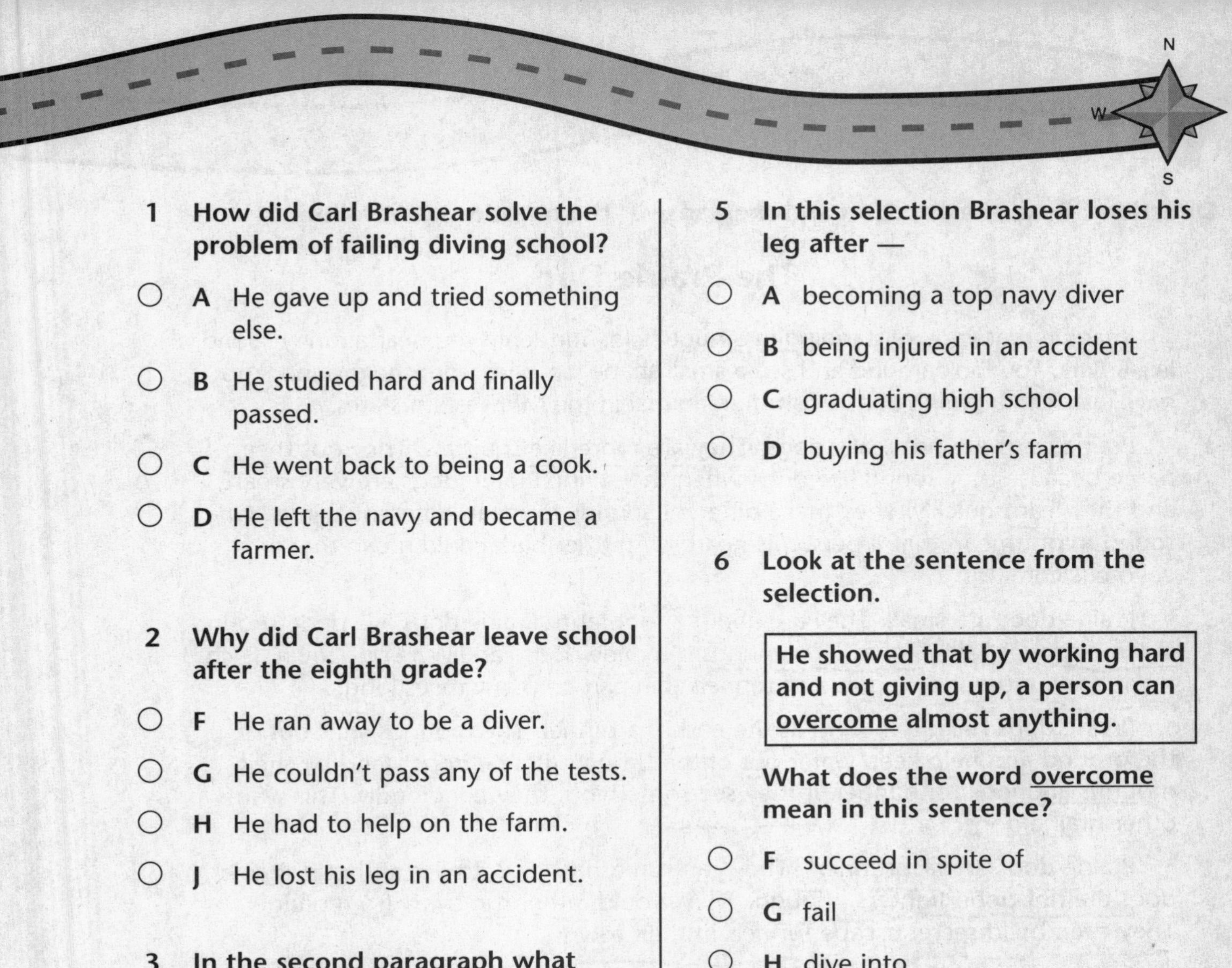

1 How did Carl Brashear solve the problem of failing diving school?

- ○ A He gave up and tried something else.
- ○ B He studied hard and finally passed.
- ○ C He went back to being a cook.
- ○ D He left the navy and became a farmer.

2 Why did Carl Brashear leave school after the eighth grade?

- ○ F He ran away to be a diver.
- ○ G He couldn't pass any of the tests.
- ○ H He had to help on the farm.
- ○ J He lost his leg in an accident.

3 In the second paragraph what does the word <u>enlisted</u> mean?

- ○ A ran away from
- ○ B failed
- ○ C got hurt in
- ○ D joined

4 Brashear had problems getting into diving school because he —

- ○ F was African American
- ○ G left school early
- ○ H was a farmer
- ○ J had one leg

5 In this selection Brashear loses his leg after —

- ○ A becoming a top navy diver
- ○ B being injured in an accident
- ○ C graduating high school
- ○ D buying his father's farm

6 Look at the sentence from the selection.

> **He showed that by working hard and not giving up, a person can <u>overcome</u> almost anything.**

What does the word <u>overcome</u> mean in this sentence?

- ○ F succeed in spite of
- ○ G fail
- ○ H dive into
- ○ J buy

7 Which word below means the same as <u>convinced</u> from paragraph 6?

- ○ A asked
- ○ B injured badly
- ○ C failed an important test
- ○ D changed the opinion

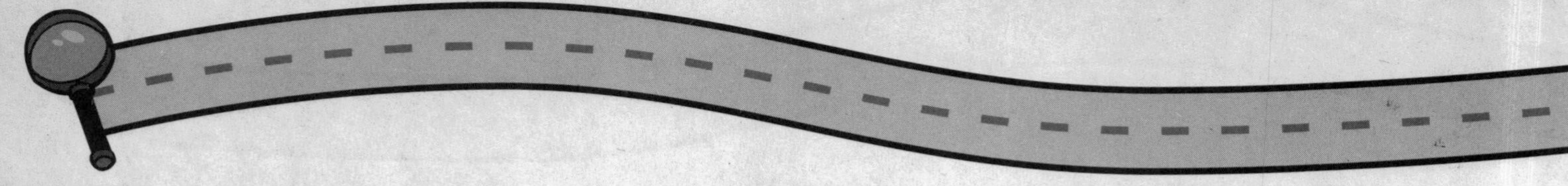

Directions: Read the selection and then answer the questions that follow.

The Prairie Dog

1 Imagine that you are standing in a huge field. Suddenly you hear a funny sound, like a bark. You look around and see a small shape jump up from the ground. You have just seen a prairie dog, a common animal in the Midwestern states.

2 Prairie dogs are not really dogs. They are more like squirrels. They got their name because they sound like dogs when they bark. Prairie dogs are very smart, and they learn quickly. They make different sounds to mean different things. One sound might mean that a person is nearby. Another bark could mean that a coyote is coming.

3 Prairie dogs are small. They are about a foot long. Prairie dogs live underground in large groups called towns. Thousands of prairie dogs can live in one town. Each town has hundreds of rooms and tunnels that can be many miles long.

4 Prairie dogs build a mound at the end of a tunnel. The mounds stick out of the ground and help keep water out of the tunnels. Prairie dogs stand by their mounds and look for danger. If they see something, they bark loudly. This warns other prairie dogs.

5 Prairie dogs are fast runners. They can run as fast as 35 miles an hour! Prairie dogs are not good fighters, though. They would rather run away from danger. They even build secret escape tunnels in their towns.

6 Prairie dogs are very active. They like to run and play games. They also stay busy by building more tunnels and rooms in their towns. Babies stay in special rooms. Mother prairie dogs watch the babies and take care of them.

7 Hawks and snakes are dangerous to prairie dogs. However, the most dangerous enemies are people. Farmers kill prairie dogs because they need their land for farming. People have killed so many prairie dogs that the animals do not live in some places anymore. If people continue to kill prairie dogs, they may all be gone someday.

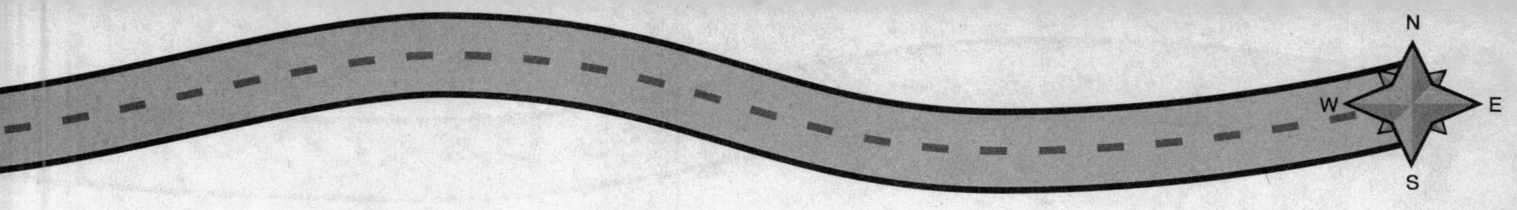

8 **In the sixth paragraph in the story, what does the word <u>active</u> mean?**

- F busy
- G mean
- H strange
- J boring

9 **Prairie dog towns are very large because —**

- A prairie dogs are very large
- B prairie dogs like to take over farms
- C prairie dogs like to be alone
- D many prairie dogs live in them

10 **Which of the answers below means the same as <u>mound</u> as it is used in paragraph 4?**

- F deep hole
- G small hill
- H fast car
- J small house

11 **Why do prairie dogs build mounds?**

- A to trap animals for food
- B to hide the baby prairie dogs
- C to scare enemies away
- D to keep water out of the tunnels

12 **Why do some people kill prairie dogs?**

- F Prairie dogs are small.
- G Prairie dogs like to run and play games.
- H Prairie dogs use up valuable farming land.
- J Prairie dogs like to chase animals and fight.

13 **Look at this sentence from the selection.**

> **One sound might mean that a person is <u>nearby</u>.**

What does the word <u>nearby</u> mean in this sentence?

- A happy
- B hungry
- C smart
- D close

14 **Prairie dogs need to be very fast to help them —**

- F catch the plants they eat
- G run away from danger
- H talk to each other
- J chase farmers away from their land

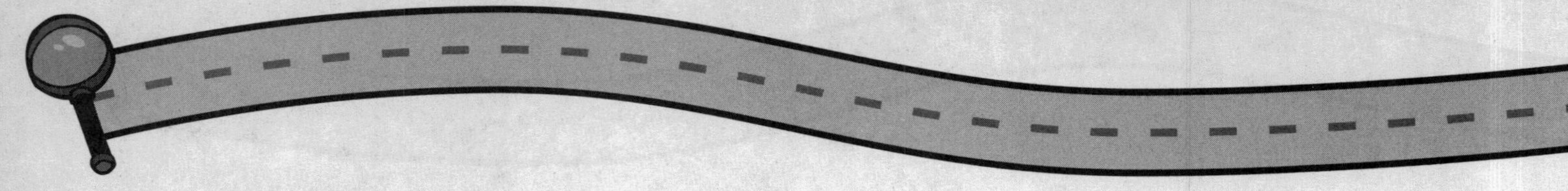

Directions: Read the selection and then answer the questions that follow.

The American Flag

1 You probably recognize the American flag. You know that it is red, white, and blue, and has stars and stripes on it. But do you know the history of our flag?

2 Many people believe that a congressman from New Jersey designed the first American flag and that Betsy Ross made the first one. However, no one knows for sure. In 1777 the flag with thirteen stripes and thirteen stars became the flag of the United States. It had one star and stripe for each of the first thirteen colonies. Since then, one star for every new state has been added. Because there are now fifty states, our flag has fifty stars. It still has only thirteen stripes.

3 Our national anthem began as a poem. Francis Scott Key wrote it in 1814. The name of the poem was "The Star-Spangled Banner." The poem was about a real flag that flew at Fort McHenry in Baltimore. Key saw the flag on a visit there. He decided to write a poem about it. Years later, someone else added music to it. You can still see the original Star-Spangled Banner. It is in the National Museum of American History in Washington, D.C.

4 Many other people have written songs and poems about our flag. Our flag is the symbol of our country. It represents our freedom.

5 There are many rules about our flag. Most people raise the flag each morning. Then they bring it down at night. However, some places fly the flag all day and night. The White House is one of those places. The flag can only be flown upside down in emergencies.

6 These are just some of the interesting facts about our flag. You can find more facts in history books. You can also look in the library. Many people have died protecting our flag and what it stands for. The next time you see an American flag, think about the new facts you have learned.

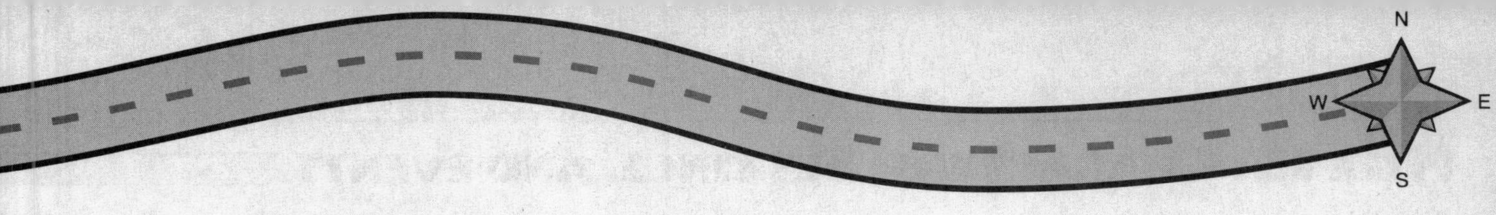

15 A star is added to the American flag when —

- ○ **A** a new state is added
- ○ **B** a war is won
- ○ **C** an original colony is created
- ○ **D** a new year begins

16 Look at this sentence from the selection.

> **You probably <u>recognize</u> the American flag.**

What does the word <u>recognize</u> mean in this sentence?

- ○ **F** know
- ○ **G** scare
- ○ **H** see
- ○ **J** enjoy

17 Why have so many people written about the American flag?

- ○ **A** They were forced to write about it.
- ○ **B** The flag makes them feel proud.
- ○ **C** They like the pretty colors.
- ○ **D** They didn't like the rules about the flag.

18 Look at the sentence from the selection.

> **Many people believe that a congressman from New Jersey <u>designed</u> the first flag.**

What does the word <u>designed</u> mean in this sentence?

- ○ **F** bought
- ○ **G** created
- ○ **H** found
- ○ **J** lifted

19 In the third paragraph of the story, what does the word <u>original</u> mean?

- ○ **A** fake
- ○ **B** late
- ○ **C** last
- ○ **D** first

20 Look at the two sentences below from the selection.

> **Our flag is the symbol of our country. It <u>represents</u> our freedom.**

What does the word <u>represents</u> mean in this sentence?

- ○ **F** gives away
- ○ **G** stands for
- ○ **H** changes
- ○ **J** loses

MILE 18: CHARACTERS, SETTINGS, AND EVENTS

A **character** in a story is a person. Every character has features that make him or her different.

Directions: Read the passage to find out what happens when a young girl goes shopping by herself.

Anika and Her New Hat

1 Anika finished her Saturday chores with a happy smile. Doing chores was boring, but the three dollars she earned each week made up for it. Anika went into her father's office and asked him for her allowance.

2 "Have you finished all of your chores?" he asked.

3 "Yes, Father," said Anika.

4 "Then here is your money. In fact, I'm going to give you an extra dollar because you did a lot of work this week. What are you going to do with all this money?"

5 Anika thought for a moment and then said, "I want to walk into town and buy a hat. Thank you, Father!" Anika kissed him goodbye and went outside.

6 Bayview was a small town and Anika was able to walk from her house to the hat store in a few minutes. When she got there, she found a note on the door that read BACK IN ONE HOUR. Anika stood on the sidewalk. Now what would she do? She decided to look into some of the other stores. That was when she noticed the new store. The sign out front read GRAND OPENING. Underneath it was another sign. It read ANYTHING YOU WANT.

7 "What an odd name for a store," thought Anika. She decided to look inside. She opened the door and walked in. It was dark inside because the store was so full of things. Everywhere Anika looked, she saw shelves piled high with stuff. Just then a man came up to her and asked her if he could help her.

8 "My name is Mr. Foley," he said. "I own this store. Now, what are you looking for?"

9 "Actually, I would like to buy a hat," said Anika. "I only have four dollars, though."

10 "I think we can find something for you," said Mr. Foley. Anika followed him down a long aisle. Finally he stopped next to a big, round box. He picked it up and handed it to Anika. Anika opened the box and inside was a beautiful hat. It was green and had a small, pink feather at the back. She tried it on and found that it was a perfect fit.

11 "I love it!" she said. "How much is it?"

12 "You are in luck," said Mr. Foley. "That hat costs three dollars."

13 Anika paid him and left the store with her new hat. As she passed the hat store, she looked in the window. To her surprise, there was a hat just like the one she had bought. The price tag on it read twenty dollars! Anika smiled as she walked home. She could not wait to tell her family about the new store in town.

Directions: Answer the following questions about the passage you have just read.

1 **Who are the characters in "Anika and Her New Hat"? Identify each character and write down an adjective that best describes each one.**

Character	Adjective
______________________	______________________
______________________	______________________
______________________	______________________

2 **Where does the story mainly take place?**

____

____

3 **When does the story take place?**

____

____

4 **What is the main problem in the story?**

____

____

5 **How is the main problem solved?**

____

____

6 **What is the lesson of this story? (Several answers could be correct.)**

____

____

Directions: Read the story below and then answer the questions on the next page.

The Fishing Trip

1 Olaf looked out the entrance of his igloo. It was early morning, and the sun was just coming up. Olaf decided that it was going to be a warm day, so he put on his light coat. He walked out of the igloo and over to his sled. The early-morning sun made the ice shine like a mirror. Olaf fed his three sled dogs and then tied them to the front of the sled. He hopped on the back and yelled "Heigh!" to get them started. The dogs raced off, snow flying up from their pounding paws.

2 Olaf was planning to spend the morning fishing. He wanted to catch some fish for dinner. He steered the dogs toward his favorite fishing spot. It was a small inlet about an hour from the village. When he got there he tied the dogs to a tree and unpacked his fishing gear. Olaf walked to the edge of the water and cast in his line. He sat down and waited for a fish to take the bait. After a few minutes, Olaf drifted off into a deep sleep.

3 A little while later he was awakened by the sound of the dogs barking. He opened his eyes, but did not see anything unusual. Suddenly he heard a strange sound. He looked at the water and saw a huge wave heading toward shore. Olaf jumped up to run away, but it was too late. The wave hit the shore like a wall of stone. Olaf was tossed into the air. For a moment he flew like a bird and saw the water below. The water was icy cold, and Olaf knew he would be in trouble if he fell into it. Just when he thought he would hit the water, he landed on something hard. To his surprise, a baby whale was in the water and he had landed on it! The whale was twice as big as Olaf. With a flip of its tail it rose up underneath Olaf. With its large head it gently pushed Olaf to shore.

4 Olaf turned around to thank the baby whale, but it was gone. Olaf walked back to his sled. Along the way he found several fish that had been washed ashore by the giant wave. Olaf loaded the fish onto the sled and got the dogs moving. He had some story to tell his family about catching these fish!

Directions: The following time lines are based on the story "The Fishing Trip." Choose your answers from the list below to complete each line. The first one has been done for you.

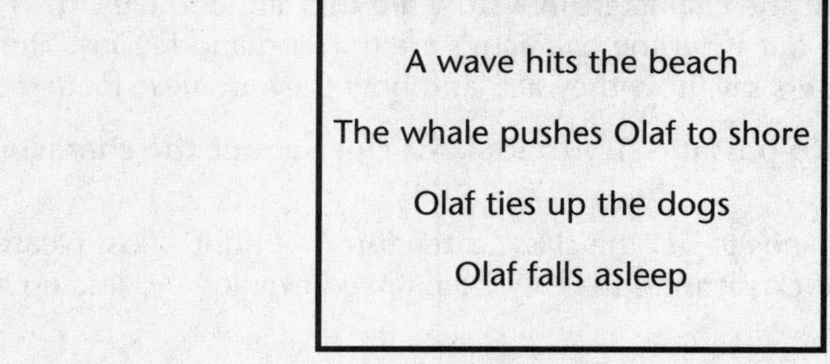

A wave hits the beach
The whale pushes Olaf to shore
Olaf ties up the dogs
Olaf falls asleep

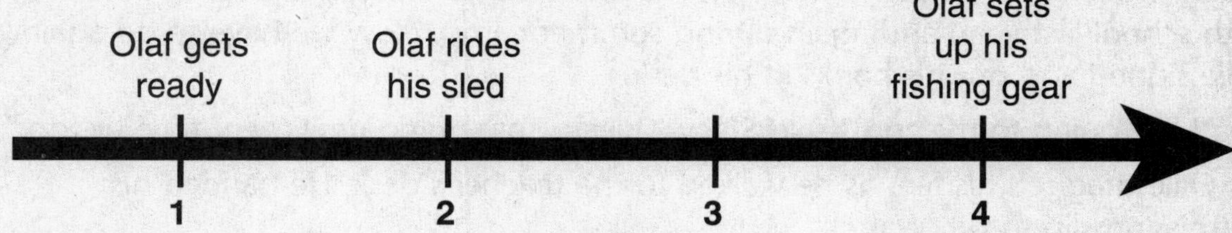

Olaf gets ready
Olaf rides his sled

7 **Which item from the list belongs in space #3?**

Olaf ties up the dogs.

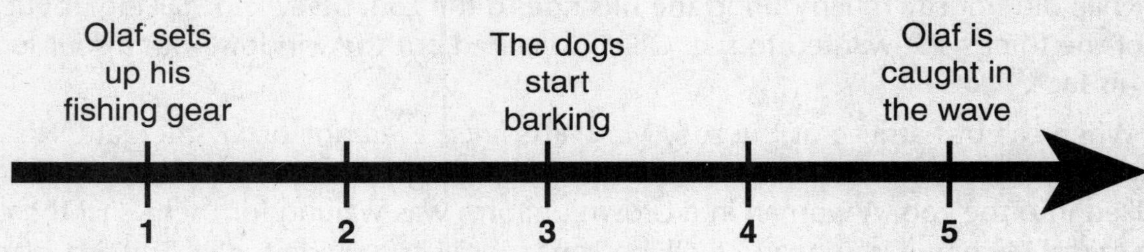

The dogs start barking
Olaf is caught in the wave

8 **Which item from the list belongs in space #2?**

9 **Which item from the list belong in space #4?**

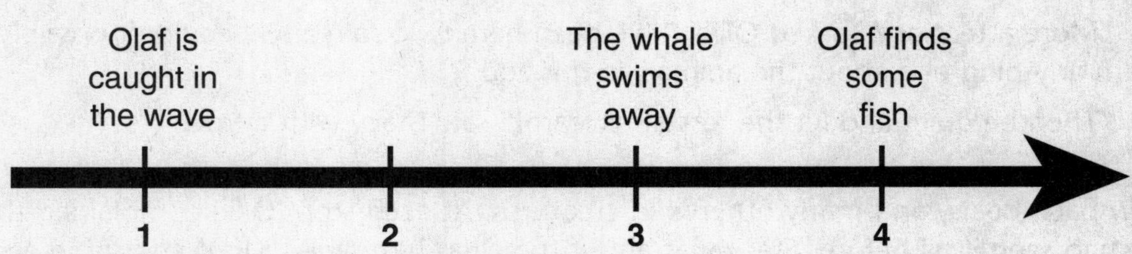

Olaf is caught in the wave
The whale swims away
Olaf finds some fish

10 **Which item from the list belongs in space #2?**

Mile 19: Getting Inside a Character's Head

Good readers think about what the characters in a story are thinking and feeling. They use clues in the story to figure out what the characters are thinking and feeling. These clues include what the characters say, how they act, and how they are described.

Directions: Read the following passage. Try to look for clues about the characters in the story.

1 Mr. Watts clapped his hands to get the class's attention. "All right, class, please listen carefully. Today is our class trip to the City Zoo. I need everyone to line up by the door."

2 Ollie turned to his friend Stacy and said, "Another trip to the zoo? We went there with school last year, and again during summer camp. Now we have to go again." Ollie sighed and put his books in his desk.

3 "I like going to the zoo," said Stacy. "I learn something new every time we go."

4 Ollie dragged his feet as he walked to the teacher's desk. He handed his permission slip to Mr. Watts.

5 "Ollie, what part of the zoo do you want to see the most?" asked Mr. Watts.

6 Ollie kept his head down as he said, "The exit."

7 Ollie did not say much during the bus ride to the zoo. Stacy kept talking about all of the things she wanted to see. Ollie just stared out the window with a sour look on his face.

8 When the bus arrived at the zoo, Mr. Watts lined everyone up by the gate. He pinned a name tag to each person's shirt. After paying the admission fee, the class walked into the zoo. A woman in a brown uniform was waiting for them. "Hi there," she said. "My name is Sue, and I will be your special zoo guide today. The first place we will visit is the elephant house."

9 Sue led the class to the elephant house. She told the students how smart elephants are. She talked about how they live in families, like people. Ollie listened for a few minutes and then said to Stacy, "How long are we going to spend in here? It smells!"

10 Stacy shushed him and said that he should be paying more attention.

11 "More attention?" asked Ollie. "I've been here twice already. I couldn't possibly learn anything else about the animals in this zoo."

12 "Then be quiet and let the rest of us learn!" said Stacy with a frown.

13 After seeing the elephants, the class walked around the rest of the zoo. They saw bats, bears, and many other wild creatures. At each stop, Ollie complained that he had seen it all before. Stacy was about to yell at him when Mr. Watts came over.

14 "Ollie, what is wrong today? You have been complaining all day long. Don't you like the zoo?"

15 Ollie did not want to get in trouble, but he couldn't lie to Mr. Watts. "I like the zoo, but this is the third time in a year that I have been here. I have heard all of these talks and seen all of these animals."

16 Sue the zoo guide heard this as well and walked over to Ollie. "I bet I know a part of the zoo you haven't seen," she said with a grin. "How about we go visit the zookeeper's area? There you can see how we fix the food for the animals and take care of sick animals."

17 Ollie's eyes grew wide when he heard this. "That would be great!" he exclaimed. Several other children, including Stacy, agreed with him. Even Mr. Watts thought it was a good idea.

18 Sue led the class to a large building. Inside it was unlike any other building at the zoo. "This is where we mix the food for the animals. Each animal gets special food. That is because not all animals eat the same thing." Sue opened one of the many doors in the hallway. Inside people were busy mixing bowls of food. Each person was looking at a list to make sure the right ingredients were used. Some of the bowls were smaller than a teacup. Others were larger than the biggest bowl in Ollie's kitchen. Sue explained that the big bowls were for animals like the lions and bears. "Now I will show you where we take care of the animals that get sick," said Sue.

19 Farther down the hall was a large set of swinging doors. The class went through the doors and into a room that looked like a giant doctor's office. There were tables that could move up and down and shelves full of medicines. A man in a white coat came up to them and said, "Hello, my name is Dr. Morris. You are just in time to see us at work." Dr. Morris explained that one of the monkeys had gotten hurt while climbing a tree. Ollie watched as the doctor put a cast on the monkey's foot. Dr. Morris told the class that the monkey would be better in a week. "Animals heal faster than people do," he said.

20 Ollie looked at Stacy and said, "I guess I was wrong. There are still things I can learn at the zoo. I can't wait to see what's next!"

Directions: Each of the following questions asks you about one of the characters in the story. Use clues from the story to help you answer each question. Go back to the story and read parts over again to help you answer the questions.

1 How does Ollie feel when he learns that the class is going to the zoo?

___

What does Ollie say or do that gives you a clue that he feels this way?

___

2 Why does Stacy tell Ollie to be quiet when they are learning about the elephants?

___

What does Stacy say or do that gives you a clue that she feels this way?

___

3 Why does Ollie finally start paying attention to what Sue is telling the class?

___

What does Ollie say or do that gives you a clue that he feels this way?

___

Directions: Below are some phrases that describe characters from the story. Write the phrase underneath the name of the character it best describes. The first one has been done for you.

Upset over the trip to the zoo

Interested in seeing the animals at the zoo

Bored with learning about zoo animals

Angry with Ollie for complaining

Happy to show the children something new

Surprised to learn something new about the zoo

Ollie	**Stacy**	**Sue the Guide**
1 *Upset over the trip to the zoo*	4 ______	6 ______
2 ______	5 ______	
3 ______		

Mile 20: Making Predictions

Making a prediction means using clues to guess what might happen next. If you see dark clouds in the sky and hear thunder, your prediction could be that it will rain. You can also make predictions when you read. Clues in a selection can help you figure out what might happen next.

Directions: Read the following passage. When you are finished, write down what you think will happen next and how the story will end. Then read the rest of the story and see how close your predictions were.

Solving a Mystery

1 Rhoda's favorite day was Tuesday. Tuesday was when she had art class. But this Tuesday was turning out differently. When she got to class, she found her teacher, Mr. Cole, talking to Ms. Nicks, the principal.

2 Ms. Nicks turned to the class and said, "I have some bad news. There will be no art class today. It seems that someone has stolen all of the paints and brushes. Until we can buy more, there will be no art classes."

3 Rhoda could not believe it! Who would do such a thing? As she sat there, she heard Ms. Nicks tell Mr. Cole that the security guard believed a student had done it. The guard said she had seen kids near the art room after school the day before. Mr. Cole said that he never locked the door to the art room because students liked to work on their projects at lunchtime. Ms. Nicks said they would probably never find out who stole the paint.

4 Rhoda decided that she would solve the case. That afternoon she went to the art room and looked around. She saw that the thieves had taken paint sets, brushes, and crayons. She thought about how the thieves had gotten away. Because the security guard had seen them after school, that meant that they had to live close by. Students who took the bus home did not usually stay after school, because if they did they would have no ride home. Rhoda knew that there were only three ways to get to the school. There were two streets and one path through the woods. She decided to walk down the path first. A path through the woods was the perfect way to go if a person did not want to be seen.

5 Rhoda began walking down the path. Right away she found a clue. At the edge of the path was a paintbrush just like the ones that had been stolen. Rhoda guessed that one of the students must have dropped it. She walked a little further and found her second clue. Someone had painted the initials "HL" on a tree in red paint. Rhoda took out a piece of paper and wrote down the initials. A few minutes later she came to a large tree with steps nailed into it. Next to the bottom step was a sign that said CLUBHOUSE, KEEP OUT! The sign was painted in the same red paint that Rhoda had seen on the other tree. She looked up and saw a big tree house. Rhoda decided that it was time to solve this mystery!

1 **What do you think Rhoda will do next?**

2 **How do you think this story will end?**

3 **What question do you think the rest of the story will help answer?**

Solving the Crime

1 Rhoda turned around and walked back to the school. Although she wanted to climb the ladder to the tree house, she thought it might be better to tell an adult first. For one thing, the students who stole the paint might be a lot bigger than she was. She also wanted to make sure that she was blaming the right people.

2 When she got back to the school, she went to the principal's office. Ms. Nicks was still there. Rhoda told her what she had seen and showed her the paintbrush that she had found. Then she told her about the initials on the tree.

3 "That's great work, Rhoda!" said Principal Nicks. "I can look in our records and see how many students have those initials. Then we can see which ones live near that tree house. You are a very good detective!"

4 Rhoda went home, pleased that she had been able to help. The next day, when she came to school, Mr. Cole stopped her in the hall. He told her how proud he was that she had helped.

5 "The principal found out that a student named Henry Logan and his friend, Mitch Ryder, built the tree house. When Principal Nicks asked them about the paint, they admitted that they had stolen it. Now they are in big trouble with their parents. You solved the mystery, Rhoda! Now we can have art class again!"

6 Rhoda thought this was the best news she had ever heard. But then he realized that she had a problem. She had always wanted to be an artist when she grew up. Now she thought that it might be just as fun to be a detective!

4 How did your predictions about the story change as you read the last part?

____

____

____

____

5 What clues in the story made you change your predictions?

____

____

____

____

6 **Write a short summary of the ending of this story.**

7 **How did the actual ending of the story compare to your predictions?**

8 **What do you think Rhoda will do next now that she has solved the mystery?**

9 **Was your question from page 85 (#3) answered by the end of story?**

Map Check 5

Directions: Read the selection and then answer the questions that follow.

Levar and His Chores

1 Levar was in his room reading a book when the phone rang. It was his best friend, Corey. "I'm going to the mall at 4:00 to see a movie," he said. "Do you want to go?"

2 "Sure," said Levar. "I'll meet you at the mall." Levar's parents had left him a list of chores to do before they left to go shopping. Levar hadn't started his chores yet. Now he had to finish them before he could leave. He hoped the list wasn't too long.

3 Levar read his list of chores and became worried. There was no way that he could finish everything in two hours. The first item on the list said, "Vacuum living room." Levar quickly ran the vacuum cleaner across the living room rug. The next item on the list was "Dust living room furniture." Levar ran a rag across all of the furniture. He did not bother to clean any pictures. He also didn't clean any shelves. The last thing on his list was "Clean your room." It was already 3:30 and his room was a mess.

4 Levar ran upstairs to his room. Instead of making the bed, he just pulled the covers up. Then he threw his toys into the closet. Finally, he pushed his dirty clothes under the bed. It was now 3:50. He had just enough time to get to the mall.

5 The movie was a fun adventure story, but Levar didn't enjoy it. He was too worried about getting in trouble for doing his chores poorly. After the movie Corey wanted to get ice cream, but Levar went home instead. He wanted to finish his chores before his parents got home. However, it was too late.

6 Levar found his parents at home waiting for him. "Your father and I are very upset," his mother told him. "You did such a poor job on your chores that I had to do them again. Now you are going to be punished."

7 Levar knew his mother was right. "We decided that you have to learn how to clean the right way," said Levar's mother. "That means for the next three Saturdays, you will have to clean the whole house. You must vacuum and dust every room and sweep out the garage. You can start with your room right now."

8 Levar went to his room and started cleaning. The more he cleaned, the more he wished he had started his chores earlier. He was going to have to get up very early on the next Saturday!

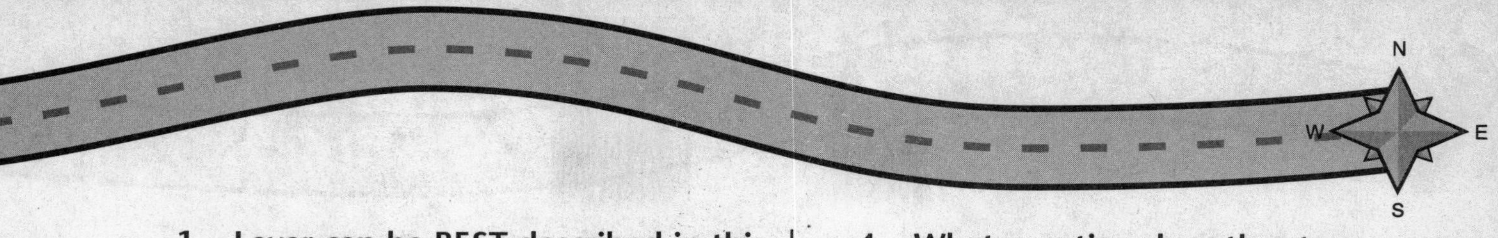
N
W
E
S

1 Levar can be BEST described in this story as —

- ○ A responsible
- ○ B smart
- ○ C foolish
- ○ D happy

2 Look at the time line below.

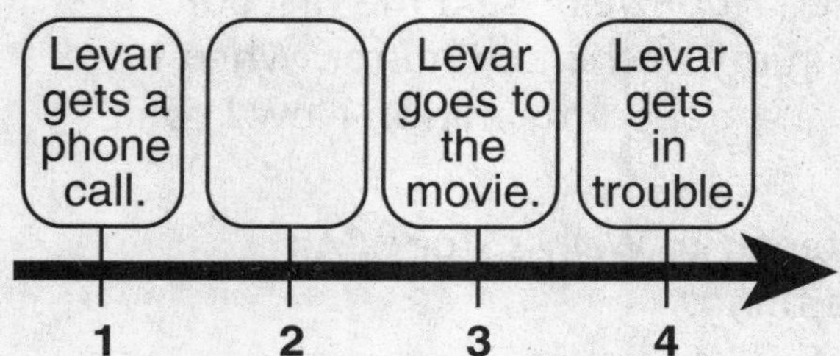
Levar gets a phone call.
Levar goes to the movie.
Levar gets in trouble.
1
2
3
4

Which answer choice belongs in the second space on the time line?

- ○ F Levar doesn't finish his chores.
- ○ G Levar finishes cleaning his room.
- ○ H Levar's mother talks to him.
- ○ J Levar does not go for ice cream.

3 In this story what is the first chore that Levar is supposed to do?

- ○ A dust the living room
- ○ B vacuum the living room
- ○ C sweep the garage
- ○ D clean his room

4 What question does the story answer in paragraph 7?

- ○ F What movie will the boys see?
- ○ G What did Levar's parents buy?
- ○ H What will Levar's punishment be?
- ○ J What time does the movie begin?

5 What did Levar do after he left the movie?

- ○ A He tried to get home before his parents.
- ○ B He went for ice cream.
- ○ C He vacuumed the living room.
- ○ D He read the list his parents left.

6 Levar probably would have enjoyed the movie if he had —

- ○ F seen it by himself
- ○ G gone shopping with his parents
- ○ H eaten ice cream afterwards
- ○ J done his chores correctly

7 What lesson do you think Levar has learned?

- ○ A Never go to a movie with your friends.
- ○ B Do not wait until the last minute to do your chores.
- ○ C Always go to the store with your parents.
- ○ D Never leave clothes under your bed.

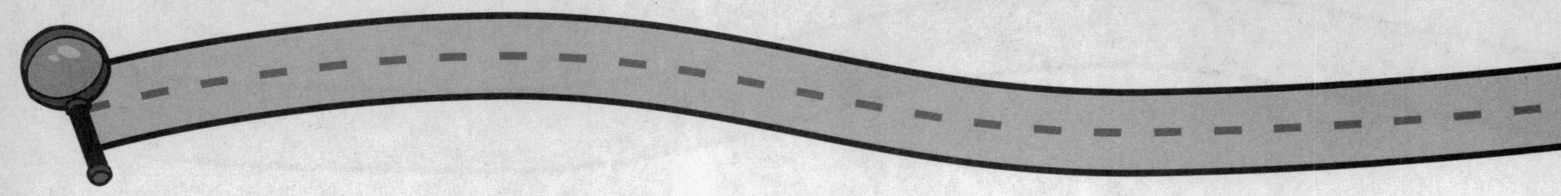

Directions: Read the selection and then answer the questions that follow.

The Enchanted Mirror

1 One day while Daniel was walking in the woods, he heard a voice. "Young man, can you help me?"

2 Daniel looked around but could not see anyone. Then he heard it again. "Please help me. I am lost." Daniel walked toward where the voice was coming from. He looked down, and on a tree stump was a raccoon.

3 "Who are you? Where do you live?" asked Daniel.

4 "My name is Wally. I come from a town called Hopewell," said the raccoon. "I was on my way home and I took a wrong turn in my enchanted mirror. When I arrived in this strange land, I was so scared that I dropped my mirror. Now I can't find it."

5 Daniel felt as if he were in a dream as he listened to Wally's story. "An enchanted mirror? I have never heard of such a thing."

6 Now Wally was surprised. "You don't have an enchanted mirror? It takes me anywhere I wish to go. Without it, I will never get back home."

7 Daniel thought about it. He wanted to see this enchanted mirror. "Okay," he told Wally. "I'll help you. Can you show me where you lost it?"

8 "Yes, I remember it well. There was a huge oak tree in front of me, the largest tree in the forest."

9 Together they set off into the woods. Wally told him about Hopewell, a magical town where animals could talk just like humans.

10 Soon they reached the huge oak and they began their search. After an hour of searching, Daniel saw something shiny in some leaves. "I found it!" he cried.

11 "I will show you how it works," said Wally. "Stare into it and think about a place you would like to go."

12 Daniel looked into the mirror and thought about his favorite ice cream shop. Suddenly, he was looking at the shop, just as if he were standing there.

13 "That is amazing!" said Daniel. Daniel handed the mirror to Wally. "I'm sorry you got lost today, but I'm glad you ended up here. I wish I could go with you to see Hopewell."

14 "But you can," said Wally. "Come with me. I will show you my town. We will use the mirror to bring you back."

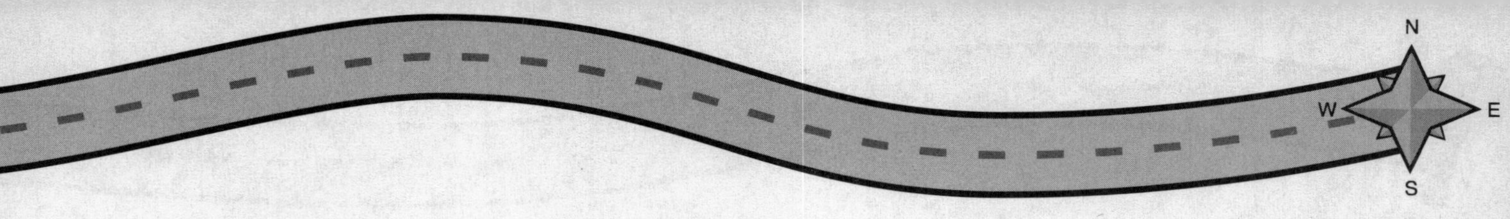

8 What is the first question that Daniel asks Wally?

- ○ F Where do you live?
- ○ G What is for dinner?
- ○ H Who are you?
- ○ J Do you have a magic mirror?

9 What did Daniel do to get the mirror to work?

- ○ A He thought about an ice cream shop.
- ○ B He rubbed it with his hand.
- ○ C He hid it in the woods.
- ○ D He asked his father for help.

10 What was Wally doing when he got lost?

- ○ F He was on his way into town.
- ○ G He was on his way to see Daniel.
- ○ H He was on his way home.
- ○ J He was on his way to see his cousin.

11 What did Daniel do to help Wally?

- ○ A He found the mirror.
- ○ B He brought him home.
- ○ C He gave him food.
- ○ D He called his parents.

12 What question does paragraph 11 answer?

- ○ F How did Daniel help Wally?
- ○ G How does the enchanted mirror work?
- ○ H Where would Daniel like to go?
- ○ J Where is Wally from?

13 What do you think Daniel will do next?

- ○ A pretend he never met Wally
- ○ B take Wally to his school
- ○ C go to the ice-cream shop
- ○ D visit Hopewell

14 Look at the time line below.

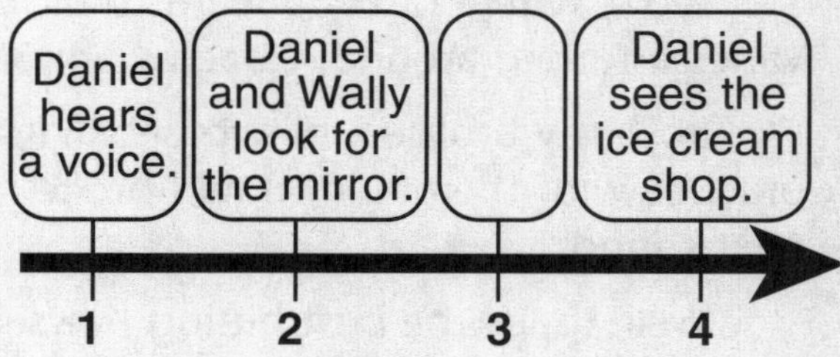

Which answer correctly fills in the third space on the time line?

- ○ F Daniel meets Wally.
- ○ G Wally tells Daniel about the mirror.
- ○ H Daniel finds the enchanted mirror.
- ○ J Wally gets lost on his way home.

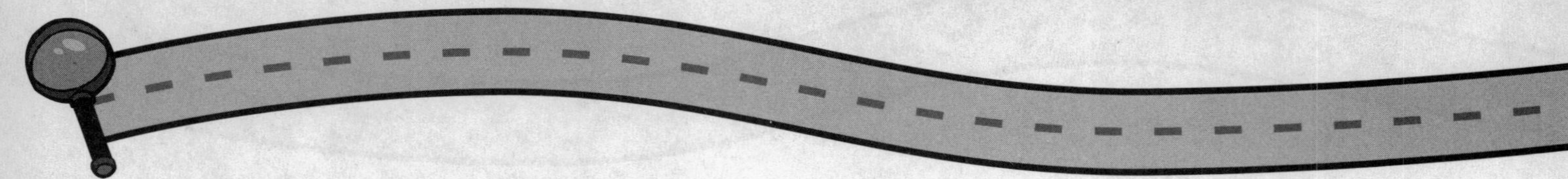

Directions: Read the selection and then answer the questions that follow.

The Softball Stars

1 Vanessa and Tonya closed their lockers and left for softball practice. Tonya was the star of the softball team. Vanessa was also a good player, but she could not play this season because she broke her leg over the summer. Still, Vanessa always went to practice with Tonya. After practice was over, they would walk home together.

2 When Vanessa and Tonya got to the field they saw the rest of the team standing around. "Where's Coach Connors?" Vanessa asked Rita, another girl on the team.

3 "Nobody knows," Rita told her. "What do you think we should do? Should we practice on our own or wait for Coach Connors?"

4 As team captain Tonya knew that the team should practice. "Let's practice. I'll pitch, and the rest of you get in the field or up to bat."

5 Vanessa watched as the team took batting practice. As she watched, she called out helpful hints to the players. After a few minutes, Tonya asked her, "Vanessa, why don't you get up to bat and show them how it's done?"

6 "Really?" said Vanessa. "That would be great!"

7 Vanessa picked up a bat and walked to the plate. Tonya threw the ball, and Vanessa hit it over the center fielder's head. She hit the next pitch into right field. Then she hit two line drives past the left fielder. She continued to hit the ball for several minutes. She never missed a pitch.

8 "Wow, where did you learn to hit like that?" said a voice from behind the plate. Vanessa turned around. Coach Connors was standing right behind her.

9 "Both my brothers play baseball in high school," replied Vanessa. "I used to practice with them a lot until I broke my leg. Now I am not allowed to run until next spring."

10 "Well, that's the best hitting I've seen in a long time. It's too bad you can't play this year. We could really use you on the team."

11 Coach Connors watched Vanessa hit a few more balls. Then the coach had an idea. She turned to Vanessa and asked, "How would you like to be my assistant coach? You could come to all the practices and help the players with their batting. You would get to come to all the games too."

12 "Really? I would love to!" said Vanessa with a smile.

13 "Yeah!" yelled Tonya. "Now we'll be teammates!"

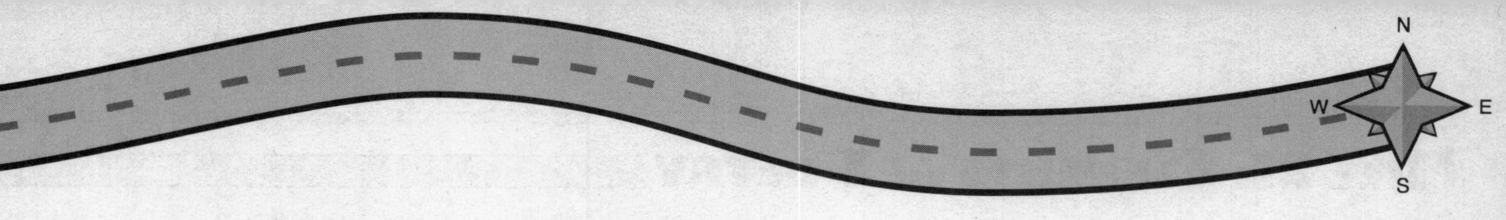

15 What did Vanessa do to help Tonya?

- ○ **A** She taught Tonya how to play softball.
- ○ **B** She told Tonya that the coach would be late.
- ○ **C** She hit balls to the team during practice.
- ○ **D** She asked the coach if she could play softball.

16 What question is answered by paragraph 9?

- ○ **F** Why was Coach Connors late?
- ○ **G** How did Vanessa and Tonya met?
- ○ **H** Where do Vanessa and Tonya live?
- ○ **J** How did Vanessa learn to hit?

17 How does Vanessa finally get on the softball team?

- ○ **A** Her brothers tell the coach how good she is.
- ○ **B** Tonya quits and Vanessa takes her place.
- ○ **C** The coach asks her to be an assistant.
- ○ **D** The coach says that her leg is good enough to run on.

18 What was Vanessa doing when the coach saw her?

- ○ **F** hitting the ball
- ○ **G** running the bases
- ○ **H** talking to Tonya
- ○ **J** doing her homework

19 What is the first thing Vanessa asks when she gets to the field?

- ○ **A** Should they wait for the coach to practice?
- ○ **B** Does Tonya want to hit some balls?
- ○ **C** Where is Rita?
- ○ **D** Where is Coach Connors?

20 What do you think Vanessa will do next?

- ○ **F** tell her parents that she is on the team
- ○ **G** tell the coach that she does not want to help
- ○ **H** tell Tonya to quit the team
- ○ **J** run around the bases

21 At the end of this story, Tonya can BEST be described as —

- ○ **A** sad
- ○ **B** excited
- ○ **C** bored
- ○ **D** frightened

Mile 21: Elements of Poetry

Poetry is one of the oldest forms of literature. People created poems even before they invented writing! Some poems describe things, and other poems tell stories. Let's look at the main parts of a poem.

A **stanza** is a section of a poem. It is usually made up of four or six lines, which are like sentences.

The **rhyme** of a poem is when some of the lines have the same ending sound.

The **rhythm** of a poem is how it sounds. Poetry can be like music. Poets sometime use certain words for certain sounds.

The **mood** of a poem is the way it feels. A poem can be happy or sad, exciting or scary. Poets use certain words to make readers feel a certain way.

The **theme** of a poem is like its main idea. It tells what the poem is mainly about.

Directions: The five major parts of a poem are listed in the box below. Each part is defined below the box. Write the word from the box that matches the definition.

Theme	Mood	Stanza	Rhyme	Rhythm

1 The feeling that a poem gives you when you read it

____

2 The main idea or purpose of a poem

____

3 When two or more words have the same or similar-sounding endings or forms

____

4 The beat or tempo of a poem

____

5 A section or verse of a poem

____

Directions: Read the poem below and then answer the questions that follow.

A Frog in the Pond

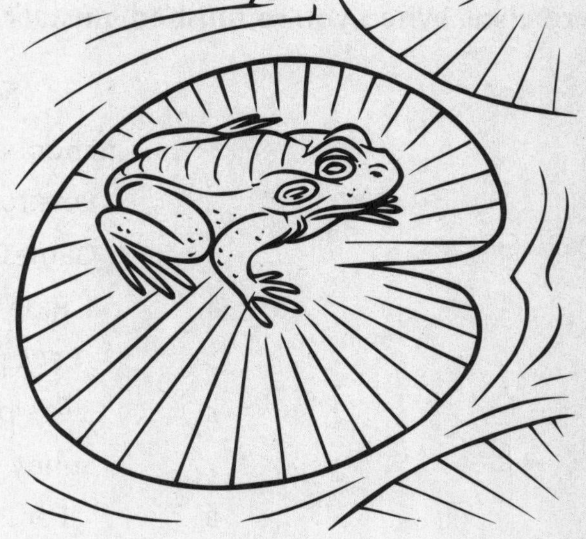

Green on top and white below,
leaping off of springy toe.
Jumping high and jumping long,
back to the place where I belong.

Into the water do I dive,
it makes me glad that I'm alive.
Swimming with the happy fish,
the pond fulfills my every wish.

The air is full of things to eat.
Flies, they are a tasty treat.
When I sit upon my lily pad,
there's no reason to be sad.

Everyone is a friend out here,
and there's only one thing that I fear.
That I'll be caught for someone's pet,
thank goodness it hasn't happened yet!

6 How many lines are in each stanza of this poem?

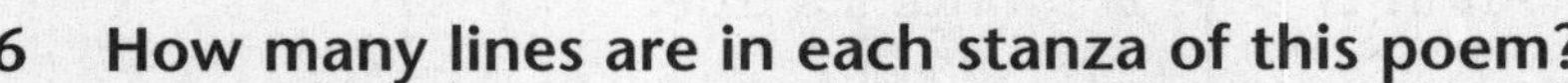

7 Which lines in each stanza rhyme with each other?

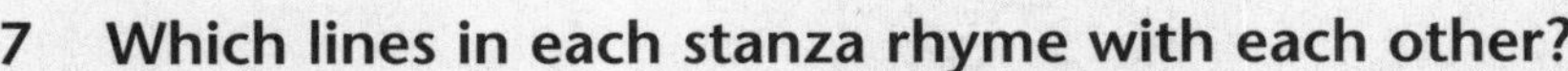

8 How does the frog feel about his pond?

9 What does the frog do or say that tells you it feels this way?

10 Which adjective below BEST describes the mood of this poem? (Circle your answer.)

Happy Sad Scary Serious Lazy

Mile 22: Making Comparisons

Directions: Read the poems on the next two pages. Look for ways that the poems are alike. When you're finished, answer the questions beginning on page 98.

Summertime

School is out, what fun, what joy.
Lots to do for each girl and boy.
Games to play and things to do,
Ride my bike, go to the zoo.
Let's play ball or catch a toad.
Let's play tag—not in the road!
Sunny days, the summer's made
For Popsicles and lemonade.
Ice cream, too, and watermelon.
A visit from my Aunt Helen.
Family picnics and barbecues.
Wearing shorts, but not my shoes!
Summer days are long, it's true.
That's why there is so much to do!

Summer Is For Kids

Summer, summer, here at last,
chill of winter fading fast.
Time to plant, time to mow,
time to watch the garden grow.
Things to do most every day,
weeds to pick, bugs to spray.
Paint the porch and clean the pool,
lots of chores, that is the rule.
Sit outside, enjoy the sun,
watch the children having fun.
Have a cookout, start the grill,
go on a picnic, better still.
Children get to run and play,
while I'm still working every day.
Time goes by so fast it seems
that summer days are gone like dreams.
Summer is for kids it's true,
adults just have too much to do.
Winter comes before you know
just where did the summer go?

Directions: Answer the following questions based on the poems you just read.

1 What topic do BOTH poems have in common?

____

____

2 How is the theme of the second poem different from the theme of the first poem?

____

____

____

3 What word BEST describes the mood of the first poem?

____

4 Which word BEST describes the mood of the second poem?

____

5 What image does the second poem use to describe how short summer days seem to be?

____

____

Directions: Look at the Venn diagram below that compares the two poems. The shared part of the circles tells about both Poem 1 and Poem 2. Answer the questions that follow. Circle the correct answer.

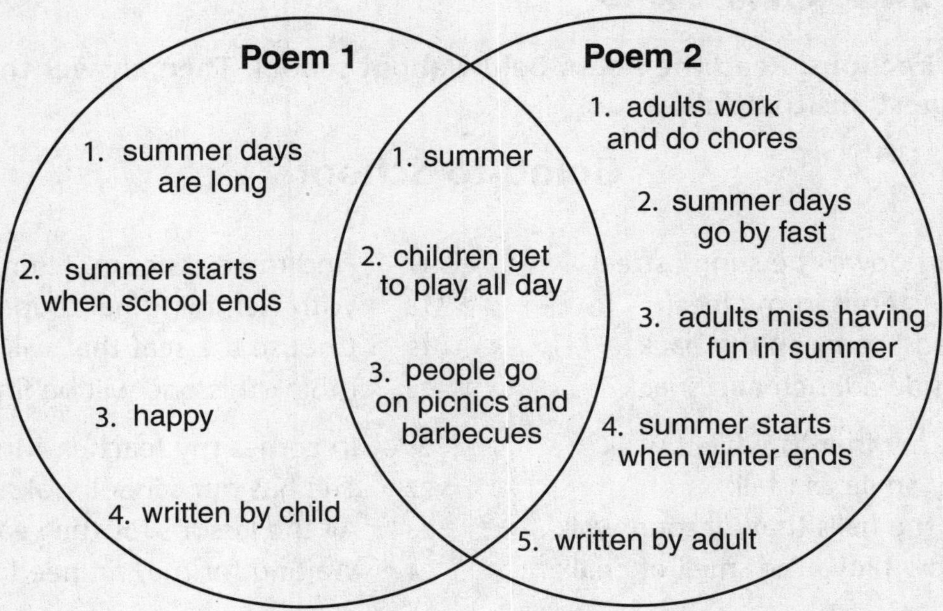
Poem 1
1. summer days are long
2. summer starts when school ends
3. happy
4. written by child
1. summer
2. children get to play all day
3. people go on picnics and barbecues
Poem 2
1. adults work and do chores
2. summer days go by fast
3. adults miss having fun in summer
4. summer starts when winter ends
5. written by adult

6 Which poem says that summer begins when winter ends?

Poem 1 Poem 2 Both

7 Which poem talks about how much fun children have in summer?

Poem 1 Poem 2 Both

8 Which poem says that summer days go by slowly?

Poem 1 Poem 2 Both

9 Which poem was written from a child's point of view?

Poem 1 Poem 2 Both

10 In which poem does the speaker seem sad?

Poem 1 Poem 2 Both

Map Check 6

Directions: Read the poem below about school. Then answer the questions that follow.

Going to School

Walking down the sunny street
A lively step is in my feet
The bag I carry on my back
Has inside a lunch and snack

I greet my friends while I walk
See me smile as I talk
About the halls that I'll soon walk
And how I love the smell of chalk

Math and science, tests so grand
Learn the history of our land
Maybe learn a language new
And why the sky is colored blue

Now up the stairs, I can't wait
Must make sure that I'm not late
Breathe the air, crisp and cool
I sure love the first day of school

Find my classroom, Number Four
With trembling hand open the door
Choose the seat that will be mine
I think this one will be fine

In comes my teacher, Mrs. Fox
She has our schoolbooks in a box
All the lessons for the year
Waiting for me, no need to fear

Poems to read, words to spell
Things that I will know so well
Games to play, math to learn
Read out loud when it's my turn

Open our books now, to page one
This is going to be so fun
Learn about a grammar rule
I sure love to go to school!

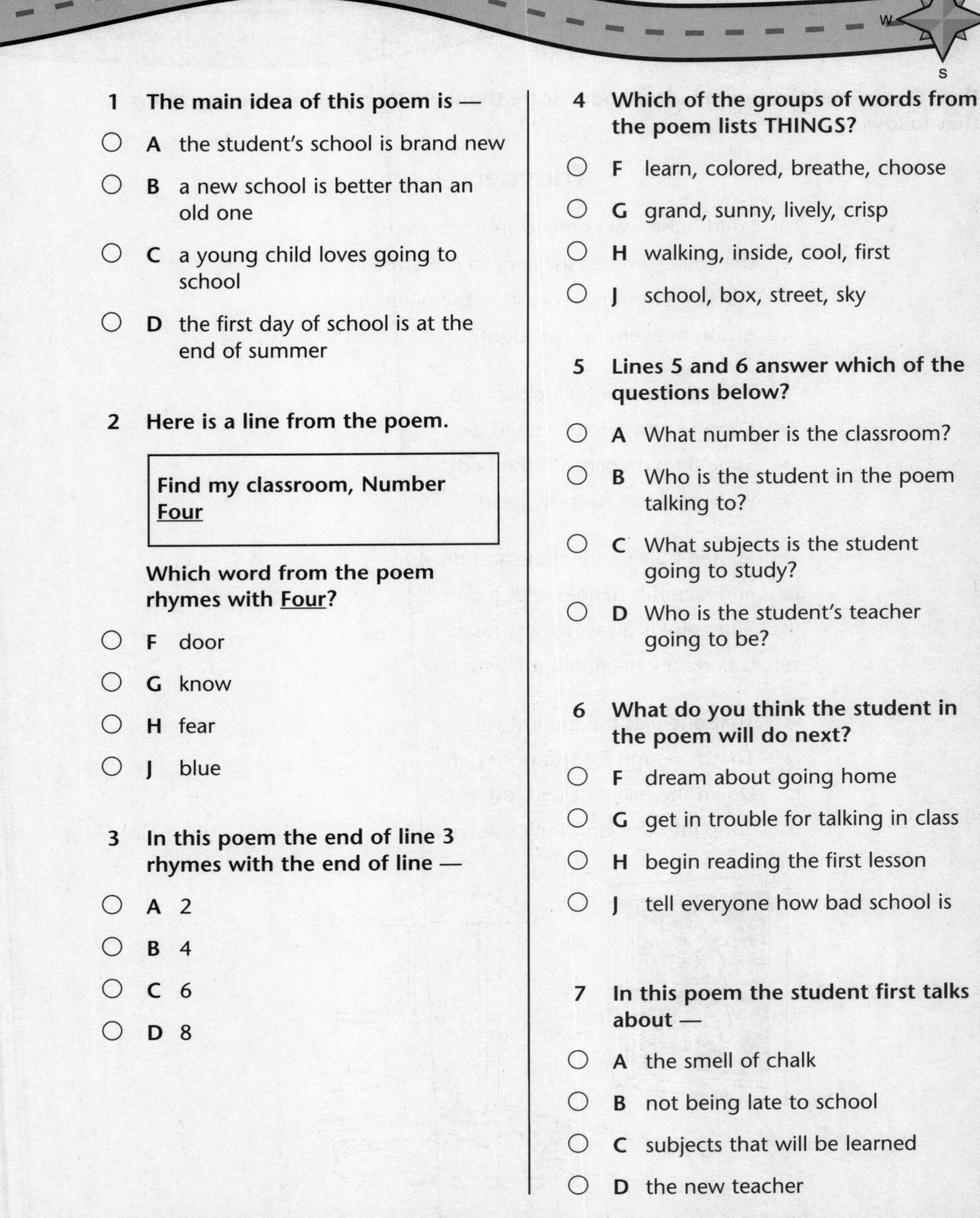

1 **The main idea of this poem is —**

○ **A** the student's school is brand new

○ **B** a new school is better than an old one

○ **C** a young child loves going to school

○ **D** the first day of school is at the end of summer

2 **Here is a line from the poem.**

Find my classroom, Number <u>Four</u>

Which word from the poem rhymes with <u>Four</u>?

○ **F** door

○ **G** know

○ **H** fear

○ **J** blue

3 **In this poem the end of line 3 rhymes with the end of line —**

○ **A** 2

○ **B** 4

○ **C** 6

○ **D** 8

4 **Which of the groups of words from the poem lists THINGS?**

○ **F** learn, colored, breathe, choose

○ **G** grand, sunny, lively, crisp

○ **H** walking, inside, cool, first

○ **J** school, box, street, sky

5 **Lines 5 and 6 answer which of the questions below?**

○ **A** What number is the classroom?

○ **B** Who is the student in the poem talking to?

○ **C** What subjects is the student going to study?

○ **D** Who is the student's teacher going to be?

6 **What do you think the student in the poem will do next?**

○ **F** dream about going home

○ **G** get in trouble for talking in class

○ **H** begin reading the first lesson

○ **J** tell everyone how bad school is

7 **In this poem the student first talks about —**

○ **A** the smell of chalk

○ **B** not being late to school

○ **C** subjects that will be learned

○ **D** the new teacher

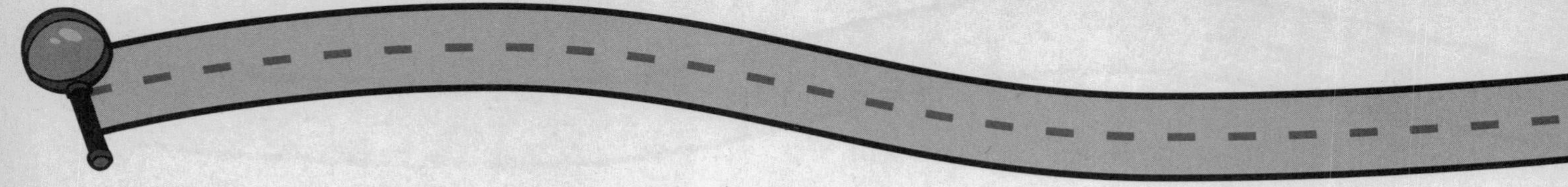

Directions: Read the poem below about scary thunder. Then answer the questions that follow.

Thunder

Loud noise wakes me from my dreams;
the whole world's shaking, so it seems.
Outside bright lights flash in the night
giving me yet another fright.

Another crash, much closer too.
I don't know what I should do.
Should I hide beneath the bed
with my paws over my head?

Should I bark and whine and howl
and face this danger with a growl?
The noise is growing ever near.
It hurts my head, fills me with fear.

That one was the loudest yet.
That's enough for this poor pet!
Down the hall, fast and faster
jump into the lap of my master!

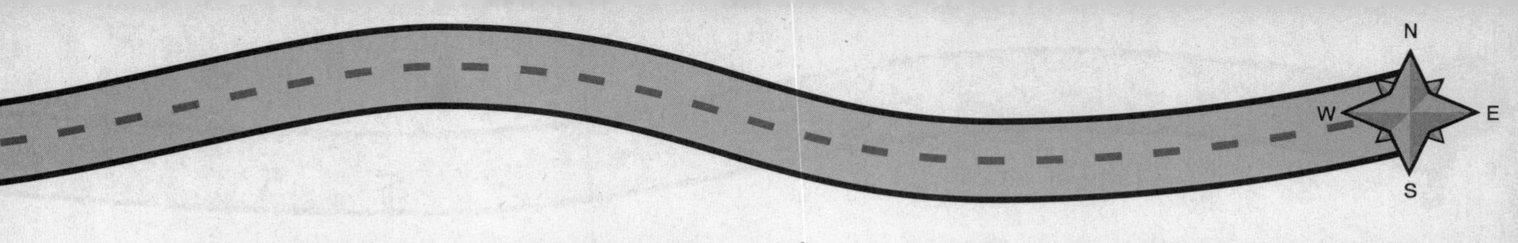

8 **Which group of words from the poem shows that ACTION is happening?**

- ○ F loud, dreams, danger, ever
- ○ G wakes, howl, hide, fills
- ○ H from, noise, another, fright
- ○ J near, fear, poor, master

9 **The main idea of this poem is —**

- ○ A a puppy is afraid of thunder
- ○ B thunder can be dangerous
- ○ C where to hide during a storm
- ○ D puppies have beds

10 **Here is a line from the poem.**

> **Should I <u>hide</u> beneath the bed with my paws over my head?**

Which one of these words below rhymes with <u>hide</u>?

- ○ F drive
- ○ G mint
- ○ H side
- ○ J climb

11 **What event in this poem does the narrator mention first?**

- ○ A running down the hall
- ○ B barking and whining
- ○ C hiding underneath the bed
- ○ D bright lights flashing

12 **What do you think the narrator of this poem will do next?**

- ○ F get its master to pet it
- ○ G run outside and bark at the storm
- ○ H hide under the bed
- ○ J bark at its master

13 **In this poem the end of line 11 rhymes with the end of line —**

- ○ A 12
- ○ B 13
- ○ C 14
- ○ D 16

14 **What question do the last two lines of this poem answer?**

- ○ F What can be done about the loud noises?
- ○ G What causes lightning and thunder?
- ○ H Where does the scared dog go during the storm?
- ○ J When will the storm be over?

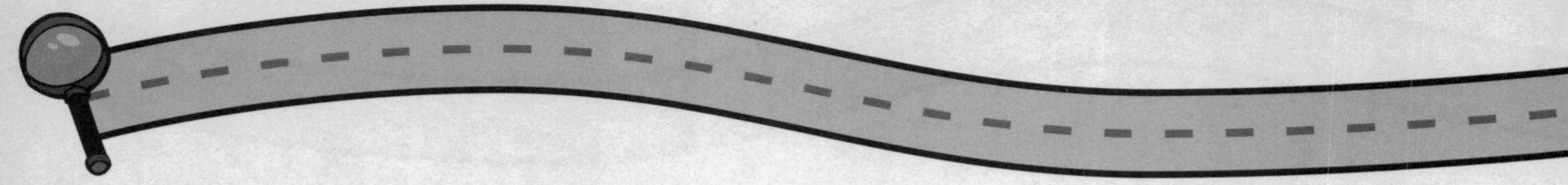

Directions: Read the poem below about a giant tree. Then answer the questions that follow.

Grandfather

A century ago and more, a seed fell to the ground
and started there a little sprout atop an earthen mound.
This little plant was shy and small, too small to even see;
who would think this tiny stem could become a mighty tree?

As years went by, the baby tree grew strong and wide and tall;
through summers warm and winters cold, through both spring and fall.
Ever higher, taller still, the tree reached toward the sky;
never stopping in its journey, no pause to wonder why.

Now the tree is older, as it stands there on its hill
towering o'er the forest, one hundred years and growing still.
I'm proud this tree is on the land that I can say is mine;
this grandfather of the forest, this tall and mighty pine.

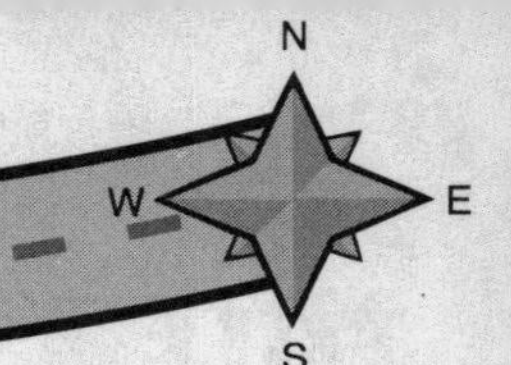

15 **Here is a line from the poem.**

> **Never stopping in its journey, no pause to wonder <u>why</u>.**

Which word from the poem rhymes with the word <u>why</u>?

- ○ **A** buy
- ○ **B** where
- ○ **C** climb
- ○ **D** tray

16 **In this poem the speaker first talks about —**

- ○ **F** how the years went by
- ○ **G** reaching for the sky
- ○ **H** when the tree was just a seed
- ○ **J** what kind of tree it is

17 **Lines 9 and 10 answer what question?**

- ○ **A** Who owns the tree?
- ○ **B** What kind of tree is it?
- ○ **C** What town is the tree in?
- ○ **D** How old is the tree?

18 **In this poem line 6 rhymes with line —**

- ○ **F** 2
- ○ **G** 3
- ○ **H** 4
- ○ **J** 5

19 **Look at the line below from the poem.**

> **A century ago and more, a <u>seed</u> fell to the ground**

Which word rhymes with the word <u>seed</u>?

- ○ **A** mound
- ○ **B** bead
- ○ **C** sprout
- ○ **D** could

20 **The main idea of the poem is —**

- ○ **F** a tiny seed grows up to be a giant tree
- ○ **G** all pine trees grow tall and old
- ○ **H** the tallest trees grow on hills
- ○ **J** trees have grandparents just like people do

21 **Which group of words from the poem contains THINGS?**

- ○ **A** seed, ground, tree, pine
- ○ **B** fell, started, earthen, grew
- ○ **C** by, strong, wide, tall
- ○ **D** wonder, older, towering, mighty

MILE 23: ALPHABETIZING

Understanding alphabetical order can help you with many tasks. It can help you find words in the dictionary or the library. There may also be a question or two about alphabetizing words on your SOL reading test at the end of the year. Writing out the alphabet can sometimes help you alphabetize a list of words.

Directions: Below is a list of eight popular books. The name of each book's author follows the name of the book. In the left column put the books in alphabetical order by the titles of the books. In the right column put the books in alphabetical order by the first letters of the authors' last names. The first example has been done for you.

Sarah, Plain and Tall —MacLachlan, Patricia

James and the Giant Peach —Dahl, Roald

Harry Potter and the Sorcerer's Stone —Rowling, J. K.

Where the Sidewalk Ends —Silverstein, Shel

Alice's Adventures in Wonderland —Carroll, Lewis

Babe: the Gallant Pig —King-Smith, Dick

Charlotte's Web —White, E. B.

Old Yeller —Gipson, Fred

BOOK TITLES	AUTHORS' NAMES
1. Alice's Adventures in Wonderland	1. Carroll, Lewis
2. ______	2. ______
3. ______	3. ______
4. ______	4. ______
5. ______	5. ______
6. ______	6. ______
7. ______	7. ______
8. ______	8. ______

1 **Here is a list of five animals. Write their names in alphabetical order on the line below.**

Horse	Cow	Mouse	Duck	Turkey

____

2 **Look at these five names. Write the names in alphabetical order on the line below.**

Tom	Richard	Moira	Alysha	Chuck

____

3 **Here are the names of five American cities. Write the names in alphabetical order on the line below.**

Detroit	Boston	Miami	Reston	Houston

____

4 **Look at these names of five different trees. Write the names in alphabetical order on the line below.**

Elm	Oak	Maple	Hickory	Birch

____

5 **Here are the names of Gail's five cats. Write their names in alphabetical order on the line below.**

Mittens	Whiskers	Snowball	Casper	Rudy

____

Mile 24: Using a Dictionary

A dictionary is a book that lists the meanings of words. It also tells you how to spell and pronounce words. A dictionary can help you understand words that you come across when you read. It can also help you find the right word when you are writing.

The **entry word** is the word that an entry is about. Entry words are listed in the dictionary in alphabetical order.

The **pronunciation** tells you how to say an entry word. The pronunciation of each word is shown after the word.

The **parts of speech** explain what kind of word the entry word is. The entry word could be a noun, a verb, an adjective, or an adverb.

The **definition** tells you the meaning of the word. Some words have more than one meaning.

An **example sentence**, which some entries will include, shows how to use the word in a sentence.

Look at this sample entry from a dictionary and look for the different parts.

cold (cold) *adj.* having a low temperature
During the winter the weather is always ***cold.***

Directions: Use the following dictionary entries to answer the questions on the next page.

deck (dĕk) *noun.* 1. the top floor of a ship. The captain walked across the deck to the sail. 2. a pack of cards.
My sister's game came with a ***deck*** *of cards.*

gab (găb) *verb.* to talk a lot
My little brother likes to ***gab*** *on the phone to his friends.*

let (lĕt) *verb.* to allow
Our teacher ***let*** *us choose our own seats.*

nice (nīs) *adj.* pleasant or considerate
The man at the candy store was very ***nice*** *to give me free gum.*

siren (sī' ren) *noun.* a warning device that makes a loud noise
The ***siren*** *on the police car was very loud.*

valley (vál'ē) *noun.* the low area between two hills or mountains
The mountains kept the cold wind from blowing into the ***valley****.*

1 What part of speech is the word ***valley***?

____

2 Which one of the words has more than one definition listed?

____

3 What does the definition of a word tell you?

____

4 What is the pronunciation for the word ***deck?***

____

5 What is a sample sentence for the word ***siren***?

____

6 What is the purpose of an example sentence?

____

7 What is the definition of the word ***gab***?

____

8 What is a dictionary used for?

____

____

Mile 25: Using a Table of Contents and an Index

A **table of contents** tells you on what page each part of a book or magazine begins. You can usually find it in the first few pages of a book or magazine. The table of contents can give lots of information, so it's good to know how to use it.

Directions: Look at the following example of a table of contents from a book about a lucky dog. Answer the six questions that follow it.

Table of Contents

Chapter 1	The Jolson Family Moves to Rocky Falls	Page 1
Chapter 2	Maria and Tino Make New Friends	Page 17
Chapter 3	First Day at a New School	Page 29
Chapter 4	Maria Finds a Surprise	Page 38
Chapter 5	A Visit to the Pet Doctor	Page 44
Chapter 6	We'll Call Him Lucky	Page 49
Chapter 7	Lucky Meets the Family	Page 53
Chapter 8	Lucky's New Trick	Page 60
Chapter 9	The Forest Fire	Page 66
Chapter 10	Lucky is a Hero	Page 77

1 **What is the title of Chapter 9?**

____

2 **What page does Chapter 8 begin on?**

____

3 **What chapter would you read to find out why Lucky is a hero?**

____

4 **Which chapter would give information on how Maria and Tino like their new school?**

____

5 **What page does Chapter 5 begin on?**

____

6 **How many chapters are in this book?**

____

An **index** tells you where to find specific information in a book. The index lists the subjects included in a book in alphabetical order. The index tells you which pages in the book have information about a specific subject. You can usually find an index at the end of a book.

Directions: Look at the following example of an index from a recipe book. Answer the questions that follow it.

L

Lasagna, 19, 30

Leftovers, 44–48

M

Meatloaf, 4–6

Mustard, 53

N

Nachos, 37

O

Oatmeal, 62

Okra, 9

P

Pasta, 19, 23, 25, 27, 30

Pastries, 77–79

Peaches, 12

Potatoes, 7, 8

7 What page would you look at to find information about peaches?

____

8 On what pages can you find information about meatloaf?

____

9 What letter would you look under in the index to find out what page in the book will tell you about oatmeal?

____

10 What food can you learn about on page 19?

____

MILE 26: USING CHARTS

Directions: Read the airport schedule below and answer the questions that follow it.

Flight Number	To	Leaves	Arrives From	Arrival Time
125	Miami	7:00 A.M.		
113			Chicago	7:15 A.M.
003			New York	8:15 A.M.
129	Boston	9:25 A.M.		
992	Los Angeles	12:30 A.M.		
828			Miami	2:00 P.M.

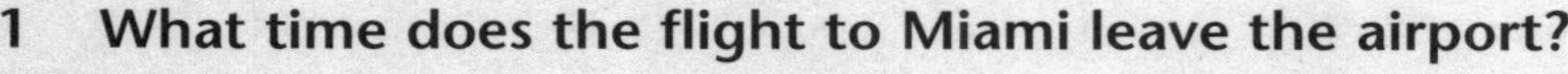

1 What time does the flight to Miami leave the airport?

____

2 What time does the flight from New York land at the airport?

____

3 What flight number would you take if you wanted to fly to Boston?

____

4 How many planes fly from this airport to Los Angeles each day?

____

Directions: In the box below is information that belongs in the chart on the page. Read the chart and then use the information from the box to fill in the blanks.

Dessert is served
Auditorium doors open
Second guest speaker
Award dinner is over

Schedule for Gopher Scouts Award Dinner

4:00 P.M.	______________________
4:30 P.M.	All guests should be seated
4:45 P.M.	Gopher Scoutmaster Wilson introduces the guest speakers
5:00 P.M.	First guest speaker
5:15 P.M.	______________________
5:30 P.M.	Dinner is served
6:30 P.M.	______________________
7:00 P.M.	Awards are announced
8:00 P.M.	______________________

Mile 27: Finding Out More

Often you will find that you need more information about a topic. Or perhaps you read a book that you enjoyed and you want to find more books by the same author. It is important that you know where to look to find the information you need.

Directions: In the box below is a list of information sources. Below the box are descriptions of each kind of information source. Write the name of the information source under its description.

almanac	atlas	dictionary
encyclopedia	thesaurus	library

1 It has articles about all sorts of different topics.

____

2 It has the definition, spelling, and pronunciation of a word.

____

3 It is filled with maps.

____

4 It shows what words have the same meaning as other words.

____

5 It is filled with facts about weather, farming, and the tides. It also contains a calendar.

____

6 It is a place to go to finds books, magazines, and recordings.

____

Directions: The following are questions that you might have while reading an article, story, or book. Write down the source that would be the best place to find the answer to each question. Use the list from page 114 to help you. You may use items from the list more than once. Some questions have several possible right answers. The first one has been done for you.

7 Where can I find more information about Native American life?

encyclopedia

8 How do I know if "barbecues" is spelled correctly?

9 Where can I find the location of Australia?

10 What is another word that means the same as "poisonous"?

11 What crops do farmers in Virginia grow during the summer?

12 Where can I find more books about lizards?

13 How do I pronounce the word "igloo"?

14 What does the word "mow" mean?

15 Where can I find information about the population of Canada?

16 In what part of the city is North Street?

Map Check 7

Directions: Read the selection and then answer the questions that follow.

Sean's First Game

1 Sean opened the closet and took out his new baseball uniform. He put it on the bed and stood back to look at it. The white and blue shirt had gray stripes on the front. The pants were solid blue. The shirt had "Bayville Sharks" written across the front. On the back it read S. Mullin, with the number 24 underneath it. Sean smiled as he looked at the uniform. It was his first one. Today he would wear it for the first time. He was now a real Little League baseball player!

2 "Sean! Hurry up and get ready. You don't want to be late for your first game!" yelled his mother. Sean looked at his clock and realized that his mother was right. He had to be at the field soon. He quickly put on the uniform, taking an extra minute to look at himself in the mirror. Then he put on his new cap and ran downstairs.

3 When he got to the ball park, some of the team members were already there. He went over to the bench and sat down. He knew that he would not get to play today because he had just joined the team. To his surprise, Coach Riley came over and said to him, "Sean, I need you to pitch today's game. Mike Chen has poison ivy and can't play." Coach Riley handed him a baseball and said, "Go get ready."

4 Sean looked at the ball in his hand. He hadn't expected to pitch today. He walked out to the mound. He tossed the ball to the catcher a few times to warm up, but he was not paying attention. He could only think about how nervous he was. When it came time for the game to start, Sean's legs where shaking. He didn't want to throw the ball. Then he saw his parents in the stands, cheering for him. He closed his eyes and took a deep breath. He opened his eyes, looked at the catcher, and threw the ball.

5 "Strike one!" yelled the umpire. Sean let out his breath with a smile. He wondered why he had ever been worried.

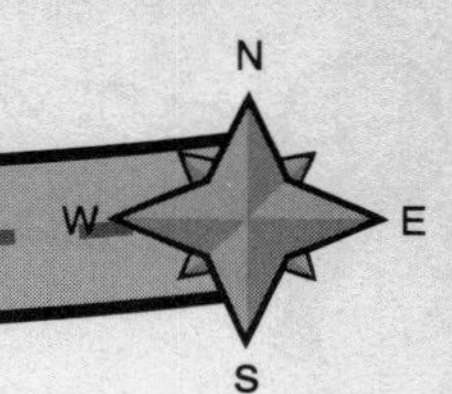

1 **Look at the picture below.**

Which line from the story does this picture illustrate?

- A "Strike one!" yelled the umpire.
- B Sean smiled as he looked at the uniform.
- C Sean looked at the ball in his hand.
- D Sean looked at his clock and realized that his mother was right.

2 **If the four words below were in alphabetical order, which word would come first?**

- F park
- G baseball
- H uniform
- J stands

3 **Why doesn't Sean pay attention when he is warming up before the game?**

- A He thinks he is too good to warm up.
- B Throwing to the catcher is boring.
- C He is looking for his parents.
- D He is scared about being in a real game.

4 **Where would you look to find more information on baseball?**

- F an encyclopedia
- G a dictionary
- H an atlas
- J a thesaurus

5 **What is the lesson that Sean learns at the end of this story?**

- A There was no reason for him to be nervous after all.
- B He should never have joined a baseball team.
- C Mike Chen got poison ivy so that Sean could pitch.
- D Throwing to the catcher was harder than he thought.

6 **What will be the next thing that Sean probably does?**

- F get scared and leave the game
- G forget how to throw the baseball
- H relax and pitch the whole game
- J ask the coach about Mike Chen

7 **What is this story's main idea?**

- A A coach has to make an important decision.
- B A new uniform is very important.
- C Baseball is a very easy game to play.
- D A boy learns not to doubt his skill at baseball.

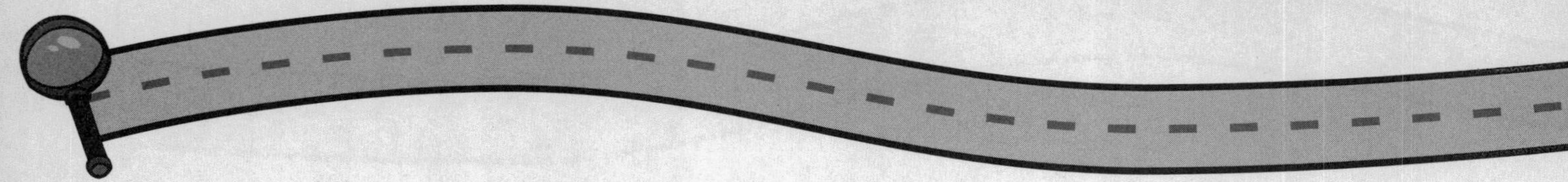

Directions: Read the selection below and then answer the questions that follow.

Dan's Best Friend

1 Every time Dan went to the mall with his parents, he stopped at the pet store. Dan wanted a puppy, but his parents felt that he was too young to have one. One day as they stood by the big window of the pet store, Dan saw the cutest puppy he had ever seen.

2 "Mom, can I have that dog?" asked Dan, pointing at a little puppy. "I really want that one, with the brown fur and pink nose."

3 "No, honey, you're still too young to have a dog," said his mother.

4 "Yes, a dog takes a lot of work," said his father. "Why don't you get a fish or a hamster so that you can learn how to take care of a small pet first?"

5 "No, I want that dog," said Dan. "I am old enough to take care of a pet. I'm nine years old now. Lots of my friends have dogs." Before his parents could say anything else, Dan ran into the pet store. He asked the clerk if he could hold the little brown puppy. As soon as he picked it up, the puppy started licking Dan's face. The puppy's tiny tail wagged back and forth. Dan looked at his parents. They could see that Dan and the puppy looked very happy together.

6 "All right, you can have the puppy," said Dan's father. "But only if you promise to take care of it, feed it, and walk it every day."

7 "I promise!" said Dan. "I can't wait to take him home. We're going to have so much fun together!" Dan and his parents picked out a little bed for the puppy to sleep on, a bowl for his food, and some toys to play with. They also got the puppy some food and a leash. The man at the pet store explained that they needed to get a license for their new dog.

8 "You are going to have to work very hard to take care of this puppy," said Dan's mother. "And part of your allowance is going to be spent on dog food."

9 "That's fine," said Dan, "but I want this puppy. I'm going to call him Brownie, and he is going to be my best friend."

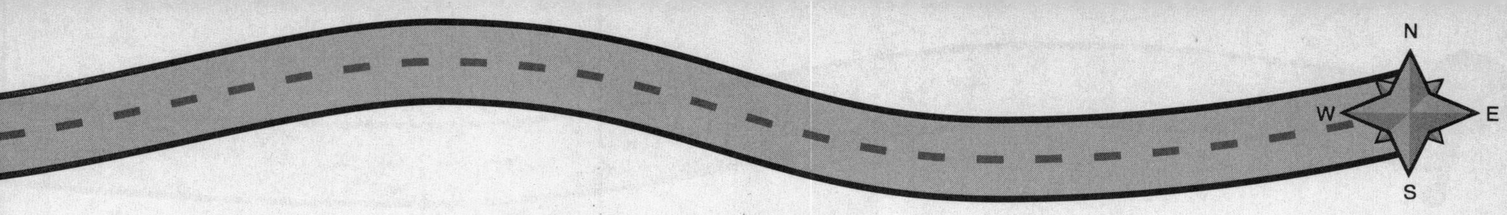

8 The main idea of this story is —

○ F a puppy runs away from home

○ G a family goes to the pet store

○ H a boy learns that he cannot take care of a dog

○ J a young boy gets a new friend

9 Look at the picture below.

What line from the story is illustrated in the picture?

○ A He asked the clerk if he could hold the little brown puppy.

○ B They also got the puppy some food and a leash.

○ C As soon as he picked it up, the puppy started licking Dan's face.

○ D I am old enough to take care of a pet.

10 If the four words listed below were in alphabetical order, which one would come first?

○ F happy

○ G puppy

○ H store

○ J leash

11 If Dan takes good care of this new puppy, his parents will probably —

○ A make him bring it back to the store

○ B let him buy a fish or a hamster

○ C trust him with other responsibilities

○ D let him open up a pet store

12 Where would be the BEST place to look to find out what the word <u>leash</u> means?

○ F an atlas

○ G a dictionary

○ H a map

○ J a thesaurus

13 Why do Dan's parents say that he should get a different pet?

○ A He already has two dogs at home.

○ B Dogs are difficult to take care of.

○ C They know that Dan is afraid of dogs.

○ D They have no money to pay for the dog.

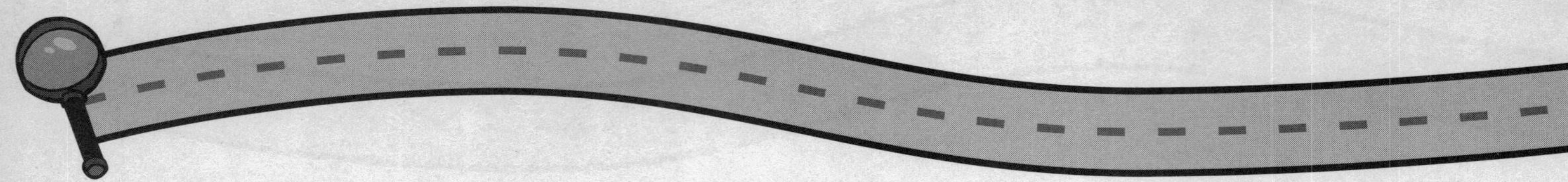

Directions: Read the selection below and then answer the questions that follow.

Carmen's Visit to Spain

1 As the giant plane began to land, Carmen felt her stomach do flips. She was about to visit Spain for two weeks! This was going to be Carmen's first trip to a new country. She could not wait to see what the cities looked like. Carmen looked at her parents and they smiled at her. Carmen smiled back. She did not want them to know that she was nervous.

2 After the plane landed Carmen and her parents got their bags. Carmen looked around, but she couldn't see anything different. This airport looked like the one in New York. People hurried from place to place. The only difference was that all of the signs were in Spanish. Carmen's father said, "Okay, let's go to our hotel."

3 Carmen's father paid a cab driver to drive them to the hotel. A book on Spain told Carmen that the money was called *pesetas*. Inside the hotel, Carmen and her parents walked to the front desk. The desk clerk looked at them and said good morning in perfect English! Carmen was surprised that people here spoke English. Her father told her that many people in Europe speak English.

4 Later that day Carmen and her parents walked around the city. They looked at tall buildings and pretty houses. There were people on the streets selling fruits and bread. She thought that was strange. People did not do that back home. Carmen bought a pastry that was better than any doughnut back home. Carmen also learned some new words. She learned that *hola* means hello. She also learned that *gracias* means thank you. Carmen was happy. She was learning how to speak Spanish! She loved learning new things.

5 For the next few days Carmen tried to learn as many new words as she could. She listened to people talking in stores. She watched Spanish television. Then one night at dinner Carmen decided to use her new words. When the waiter asked her what she wanted, she told him in Spanish. The waiter smiled and told her that she spoke Spanish very well.

6 Carmen's parents were surprised. They asked her how she learned all those words. When she said she learned from listening to Spanish people, they said she was very smart. "Maybe when you grow up, you can teach Spanish to American children," said her father. Carmen thought about it. Maybe she would.

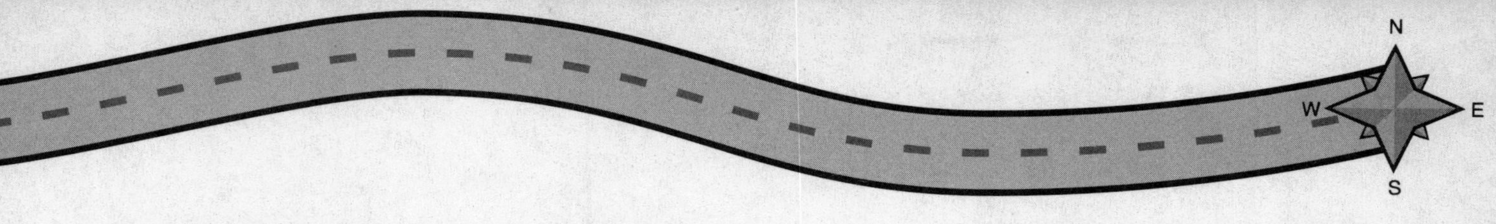

14 Where could you look to find out where Spain is located?

○ **F** an atlas

○ **G** a dictionary

○ **H** a thesaurus

○ **J** a math book

15 The main idea of this story is —

○ **A** a family learns that people in Spain speak English

○ **B** a young girl learns to speak a new language

○ **C** restaurants in Spain are very nice

○ **D** airports in Spain and America look the same

16 Why is Carmen happy?

○ **F** She is learning something new.

○ **G** Her parents took her to dinner.

○ **H** She will be going home soon.

○ **J** She enjoyed the airplane ride.

17 What do you think Carmen will do when she gets home?

○ **A** ask her parents to learn French

○ **B** buy a book of Spanish words

○ **C** learn to fly a plane

○ **D** clean her bedroom

18 What does Carmen learn in this story?

○ **F** Her family is from Spain.

○ **G** Her school does not teach Spanish.

○ **H** She is good at learning new words.

○ **J** She can teach people English.

19 If the four words below were in alphabetical order, which one would come last?

○ **A** listened

○ **B** dinner

○ **C** waiter

○ **D** teach

20 If her family stays in Spain for another two weeks, Carmen will probably —

○ **F** want to go back to America

○ **G** try to become an English teacher

○ **H** forget all the words she has learned

○ **J** learn to speak Spanish very well

PRACTICE TESTS

Introduction to the Practice Tests

You've finished all of the miles in this book. That means you've practiced all of the important third-grade reading skills. Way to go!

To check your answers to questions in the miles, turn to page 167. It may help to have a parent or teacher go throught the answers with you.

When you're ready, it's time to take the practice tests. The practice tests in this book are similar to the Grade 3 Virginia SOL English: Reading test.

On the actual Virginia SOL Reading test, you will mark your answers to the questions on a separate answer sheet with a pencil.

How to Take the Practice Tests

The answer sheet for Practice Test 1 is on the next page. The answer sheet for Practice Test 2 is on page 139. The answer sheet for Practice Test 3 is on page 153. Before you take each practice test, tear out the answer sheet that goes with it. You can cut it out with a pair of scissors if you want to.

Take each practice test as if it were the actual Virginia SOL test. That means you should not have any books open while taking these tests. Take one whole practice test at a time. If you begin a practice test, don't stop until you are finished with it. Since the Virginia SOL test is untimed, you can take as much time as you need to finish each practice test. You should not watch television, talk on the phone, or listen to music while you take the tests.

Remember to use the skills that you have learned and practiced in this book. They will help you to do your best. After you have taken each test, have an adult go over it. The answers and explanations to the practice tests begin on page 185. Pay special attention to the explanations of questions that you found hard to answer.

Good luck!

Completely darken bubbles with a No. 2 pencil. If you make a mistake, be sure to erase mark completely. Erase all stray marks.

1. YOUR NAME: ______ Last ______ First ______ M.I.
(Print)

SIGNATURE: ______ DATE: ___/___/___

HOME ADDRESS: ______ Number
(Print)

______ City ______ State ______ Zip Code

PHONE NO.: ______
(Print)

2. YOUR NAME

First 4 letters of last name				FIRST INIT	MID INIT
A	A	A	A	A	A
B	B	B	B	B	B
C	C	C	C	C	C
D	D	D	D	D	D
E	E	E	E	E	E
F	F	F	F	F	F
G	G	G	G	G	G
H	H	H	H	H	H
I	I	I	I	I	I
J	J	J	J	J	J
K	K	K	K	K	K
L	L	L	L	L	L
M	M	M	M	M	M
N	N	N	N	N	N
O	O	O	O	O	O
P	P	P	P	P	P
Q	Q	Q	Q	Q	Q
R	R	R	R	R	R
S	S	S	S	S	S
T	T	T	T	T	T
U	U	U	U	U	U
V	V	V	V	V	V
W	W	W	W	W	W
X	X	X	X	X	X
Y	Y	Y	Y	Y	Y
Z	Z	Z	Z	Z	Z

3. DATE OF BIRTH

Month	Day		Year			
JAN						
FEB						
MAR	0	0	0	0	0	0
APR	1	1	1	1	1	1
MAY	2	2	2	2	2	2
JUN	3	3	3	3	3	3
JUL		4	4	4	4	4
AUG		5	5	5	5	5
SEP		6	6	6	6	6
OCT		7	7	7	7	7
NOV		8	8	8	8	8
DEC		9	9	9	9	9

The Princeton Review

4. SEX
- MALE
- FEMALE

Practice Test 1

1. A B C D	8. F G H J	15. A B C D	22. F G H J	29. A B C D
2. F G H J	9. A B C D	16. F G H J	23. A B C D	30. F G H J
3. A B C D	10. F G H J	17. A B C D	24. F G H J	31. A B C D
4. F G H J	11. A B C D	18. F G H J	25. A B C D	32. F G H J
5. A B C D	12. F G H J	19. A B C D	26. F G H J	33. A B C D
6. F G H J	13. A B C D	20. F G H J	27. A B C D	34. F G H J
7. A B C D	14. F G H J	21. A B C D	28. F G H J	35. A B C D

PRACTICE VIRGINIA SOL READING TEST 1

Guarding the Sheep

1 There once was a farmer who raised sheep. In the mornings he would lead them from the barn to their field. There he would watch over them all day. In the evenings he would lead them back to the barn. As time went by the flock grew larger. One day the farmer realized that he was getting too old to take care of the sheep by himself. He decided that he needed a guard dog to help him.

2 The next day the farmer brought Milo home. Milo was a trained guard dog. The farmer took Milo with him in the morning. He watched as Milo walked around the field, keeping an eye on the sheep. The farmer went back to his farmhouse, happy that Milo was doing a good job.

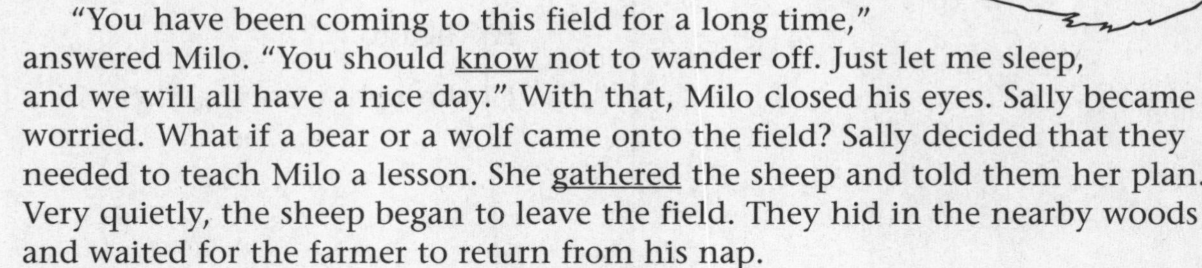

3 As soon as the farmer went inside, Milo lay down and closed his eyes. One of the sheep, Sally, came up to him and asked him what he was doing. "Why, I am taking a nap," he replied.

4 "But you are supposed to be guarding us," said Sally. Sally was the oldest of the sheep.

5 "You have been coming to this field for a long time," answered Milo. "You should <u>know</u> not to wander off. Just let me sleep, and we will all have a nice day." With that, Milo closed his eyes. Sally became worried. What if a bear or a wolf came onto the field? Sally decided that they needed to teach Milo a lesson. She <u>gathered</u> the sheep and told them her plan. Very quietly, the sheep began to leave the field. They hid in the nearby woods and waited for the farmer to return from his nap.

6 When the farmer returned, he saw Milo sleeping. "Wake up, you lazy dog!" the farmer shouted. "All of my sheep have disappeared while you were sleeping!" Milo saw the empty field and got very frightened. After a few minutes Sally and the other sheep came out of the woods. The farmer was very happy, and he led the sheep back to the barn. Then he told Milo, "Tonight you can sleep outside with no dinner. Maybe tomorrow you will remember to stay awake."

7 After the farmer went to bed, Milo asked Sally, "Why did you get me in trouble?"

8 Sally told him, "Because you are supposed to protect us. You cannot do that if you are asleep."

9 Milo agreed, and said that from now on he would stay awake. This was the last night he wanted to spend hungry and cold.

Go to next page

1 **Which of the sentences below tells what lesson Milo learned?**

A The sheep are smarter than the farmer.

B It is important for him to guard the sheep.

C Sally does not want to be his friend.

D There are bears in the woods near the field.

2 **This story is a —**

F folktale

G ghost story

H history lesson

J true story

3 **Look at the sentence from the story.**

> **"You should <u>know</u> not to wander off."**

Which of the following words rhymes with <u>know</u>?

A how

B threw

C cat

D toe

4 **In this story what does the word <u>gathered</u> mean in paragraph 5?**

F sent away

G slowly counted

H lied to

J brought close together

Go to next page

5 Here are four words from the story.

sheep, farmer, Sally, Milo

Which answer choice has all four words in alphabetical order?

A farmer, Milo, Sally, sheep

B farmer, Milo, sheep, Sally

C Milo, Sally, farmer, sheep

D Sally, sheep, farmer, Milo

6 What would be the BEST way to describe Sally?

F evil

G dangerous

H smart

J tired

7 The main idea of this story is —

A a lazy dog learns a lesson

B a good watchdog gets into trouble

C a farmer decides to get a dog

D a sheep learns a lesson about running away

8 What will Milo most likely do next?

F fall asleep in the field again

G stay in the barn while the farmer watches the sheep

H do something to get Sally in trouble

J stay awake while he watches the sheep

Go to next page

Making Money

1 You see quarters, dimes, nickels, and pennies every day. Coins are money, just like dollar bills. You use them to buy things. You put them in your piggy bank and save them. But have you ever wondered how coins are made? A mint is a special building where coins are made. There are U.S. mints in West Point, Denver, Philadelphia, and San Francisco. The headquarters for the U.S. mints is in Washington, D.C.

2 There are many steps involved in making a coin. First, an artist has to make a big drawing of the coin. Then another artist makes a big plastic model of the coin. This model is put on a special machine called an engraver. The machine carves the details from the plastic model onto a piece of metal that is the size of a coin. People inspect this metal model, called a die, to make sure that it is perfect.

3 The next step is to make the real coins. A machine cuts coin-sized pieces out of big metal sheets, just like a cookie cutter. The pieces are then heated to make them soft. The soft metal pieces are stamped by the dies and turned into coins. An inspector <u>examines</u> some coins from each batch and makes sure that the coins are being made correctly. Then a machine counts the coins and wraps them. They are put into bags and delivered to banks.

4 If you look closely at a coin, you may see a special mark on the front. This mark tells what mint it is from. On the back you can find the designer's initials. The next time you look at a coin, think about all the work that went into making it.

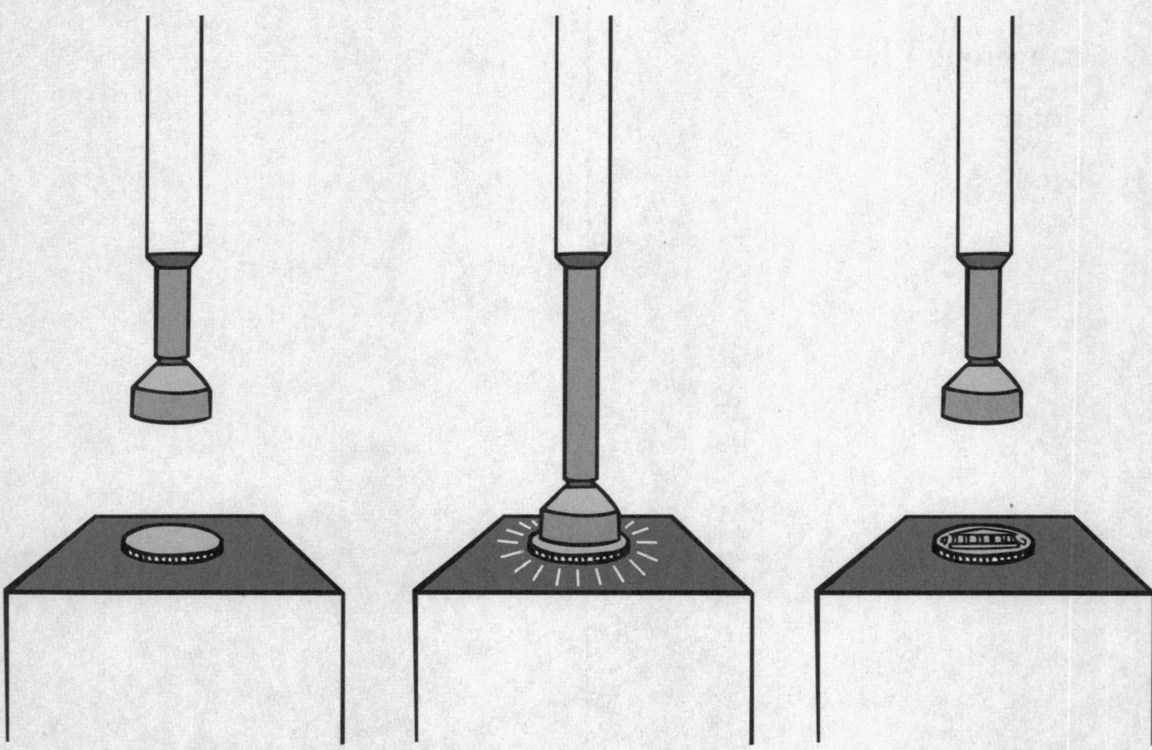

Go to next page

9 **A good place to find more information on making coins would be —**

A a thesaurus

B an encyclopedia

C a dictionary

D a biography

10 **Look at the four boxes below.**

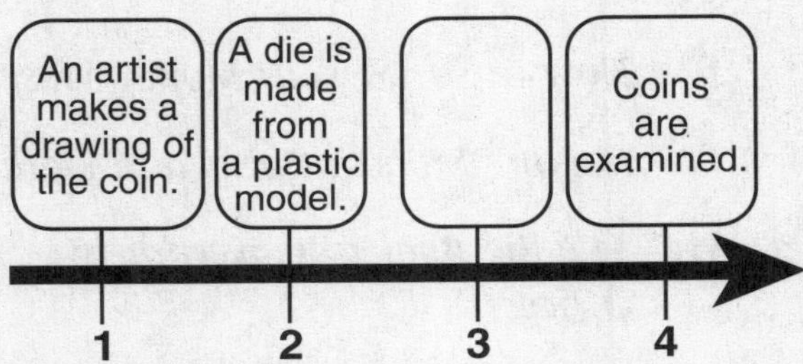

Which of these answers belongs in box number 3?

F An artist makes a plastic model of the coin.

G A machine counts and wraps the coins.

H The blank metal is stamped.

J The coins are sent to banks.

11 **What is the meaning of the word <u>examines</u> in paragraph 3?**

A looks at

B count

C plays with

D steals

12 **Look at the sentence from the article about coins.**

> **"<u>Coins</u> are money, just like dollar bills."**

Which of the following words has a sound like the "c" in <u>coins</u>?

F chew

G gold

H change

J kid

Go to next page

13 It is a difficult process to make coins because —

A they are made in only one place

B there are many detailed steps

C all the different coins look the same

D they are made out of plastic

14 Read the following sentences about making money. Then select the answer that best fills in the blanks.

A penny is equal to one _______. A dollar equals _______ hundred pennies.

F scent, won

G cent, won

H scent, one

J cent, one

15 The answer to what question is found in paragraph 1?

A Where are coins made?

B What are coins made of?

C What do the marks on coins mean?

D How a dollar bill is printed?

16 To find out more about mints, the BEST book to read would be —

F *How to Spend Your Money Wisely*

G *Making Money: Coins and Dollars*

H *The Big Book of Government Offices*

J *Gold Coins: Buried Treasure in the Sea*

Go to next page

Underwater Pioneer

1 The man flew through the water like a bird. He was the first person to dive in the ocean without an airhose connected to a boat. He was wearing a special air tank on his back. Jacques Cousteau was now the very first scuba diver.

2 Jacques Cousteau was a French navy officer. He had always loved swimming in the ocean. Even when he was a little boy, he would swim and watch the fish. As he grew older, his love of the ocean grew even stronger. He began to invent things to help him dive better. He built special diving glasses. He did this so he could see better underwater. He also built the first movie camera that worked underwater. This let him film all of the amazing animals he saw on his dives.

3 He still needed to <u>solve</u> one final problem, though. He had to find a way to breathe underwater. At the time that he was diving, divers had to wear heavy suits filled with air. The air came from a hose attached to a pump on a boat. The pump sent air through the hose and into the suit. The suits were so heavy that people could not swim in them. Instead, they had to walk on the ocean bottom.

4 Cousteau and a man named Emile Gagnan invented the scuba tank. The tank was filled with air and connected to a face mask by a hose. A diver could wear the tank on his back. Cousteau and Gagnan called it the Aqua-lung. The Aqua-lung allowed Cousteau to swim underwater with his movie camera. No longer did a diver have to depend on a boat for air. With his tanks, Cousteau began diving as deep as 210 feet under the water.

5 In 1957 he made his first movie, *The Silent World*. It was so popular that it won an Academy Award. Cousteau produced more than a hundred films. He won two more Academy Awards. He also won many awards for his television specials. Cousteau traveled around the world in a special boat. He and his crew filmed everything they saw on their dives. They made films about sharks, whales, and coral reefs. Although he died in 1997, his work is still going strong today. Before he died, he started The Cousteau Society. It is dedicated to protecting the oceans and the plants and animals that live in them.

Go to next page

17 Look at the sentence below from the story about Jacques Cousteau.

No longer did a diver have to depend on a boat for air.

Which sentence below means the same thing as the above sentence?

A Divers no longer had to depend on air.

B Divers did not have air any longer.

C Divers did not need to depend on a boat for air.

D Divers did not need to travel in boats anymore.

18 Look at the picture below.

Which of the words below rhymes with the word for what is shown in the picture above?

F wish

G test

H push

J list

19 In paragraph 3 the word <u>solve</u> means —

A question

B find the answer to

C take a test about

D make

20 Look at the two sentences about the Underwater Pioneer.

Jacques Cousteau studied the _____. He also _____ many movies about his travels.

Which pair of words correctly fills in the blanks?

F see, made

G sea, maid

H see, maid

J sea, made

21 The Cousteau Society probably —

A does not exist anymore

B sells diving equipment and boats

C still makes movies about the oceans

D takes people on long fishing trips

Go to next page

22 What is the BEST way to describe Jacques Cousteau?

F silly, angry, and frightened

G daring, brave, and curious

H dull, boring, and lazy

J calm, happy, and clumsy

23 To find out more information about scuba divers, the BEST source to look in would be —

A an encyclopedia

B a dictionary

C a math book

D an atlas

24 What was the last problem Cousteau had to solve before he could dive the way he wanted to?

F He had to learn how to swim with fins on.

G He had to invent glasses so that he could see underwater.

H He had to find a way to breathe underwater.

J He had to start The Cousteau Society.

25 What type of a story is "Underwater Pioneer"?

A fairytale

B biography

C poem

D fable

Go to next page

Finally Spring

Joyful feelings in the air,
People laugh and sing;
Happy faces everywhere,
As we enjoy the spring.
Wander down the busy streets,
With gifts to share and bring;
Oh how fun to be a child,
When it's time for spring.

Breezes blow, robins chirp,
Bells just seem to ring;
We will play in baby grass,
The carpet of the spring.
Every plant so fresh and new,
As the sun feeds everything;
Nature puts her coat away,
When winter turns to spring.

Fishing rods, flying kites,
Balls to catch and fling;
Oh the games children play,
In the season we call spring.
Joyful people everywhere,
Hear them laugh and sing;
Happy faces, not a care,
As we enjoy the spring.

Go to next page

26 Which of the following answers rhymes with kite?

F might

G crate

H bit

J seat

27 Read line 4 from the poem.

As we enjoy the spring.

The word spring rhymes with the last word of which line in the poem?

A 1

B 3

C 5

D 6

28 Which list below has words from the poem listed in alphabetical order?

F air, spring, chirp, people

G chirp, spring, air, people

H air, chirp, people, spring

J spring, people, chirp, air

29 Which answer choice describes the main idea of the poem?

A People like to play games when the weather is cold.

B Everyone is happy when winter is over and spring has arrived.

C Many plants that cannot grow in the winter can grow when spring arrives.

D Winters are always long and cold, and nobody likes the season.

30 Lines 17 through 20 tell about —

F games people like to play in the spring

G how Mother Nature gets ready for spring

H all the happy people in the streets

J how it is time to put away winter coats

Go to next page

31 What do the joyful people in the poem do?

A feed everything

B put their coats away

C stay inside

D laugh and sing

32 What are the children in the poem most likely going to do next?

F put on coats

G ride bicycles

H stay inside

J make snowballs

33 In line 5 of this poem, what does the word <u>wander</u> mean?

A move slowly

B stay in one place

C fly kites

D get dressed

34 Look at the picture below.

What line from the poem does the picture illustrate?

F Wander down the busy streets

G People laugh and sing

H We will play in baby grass

J Balls to catch and fling

35 Read these two lines from the poem.

Oh how fun to be a child, **When <u>it's</u> time for spring.**

What is a different way of writing <u>it's</u>?

A it has

B it is

C it will

D is not

Completely darken bubbles with a No. 2 pencil. If you make a mistake, be sure to erase mark completely. Erase all stray marks.

1. YOUR NAME: ______ (Print) Last First M.I.

SIGNATURE: ______ DATE: / /

HOME ADDRESS: ______ (Print) Number

______ City State Zip Code

PHONE NO.: ______ (Print)

2. YOUR NAME

First 4 letters of last name				FIRST INIT	MID INIT
A	A	A	A	A	A
B	B	B	B	B	B
C	C	C	C	C	C
D	D	D	D	D	D
E	E	E	E	E	E
F	F	F	F	F	F
G	G	G	G	G	G
H	H	H	H	H	H
I	I	I	I	I	I
J	J	J	J	J	J
K	K	K	K	K	K
L	L	L	L	L	L
M	M	M	M	M	M
N	N	N	N	N	N
O	O	O	O	O	O
P	P	P	P	P	P
Q	Q	Q	Q	Q	Q
R	R	R	R	R	R
S	S	S	S	S	S
T	T	T	T	T	T
U	U	U	U	U	U
V	V	V	V	V	V
W	W	W	W	W	W
X	X	X	X	X	X
Y	Y	Y	Y	Y	Y
Z	Z	Z	Z	Z	Z

3. DATE OF BIRTH

Month	Day		Year			
JAN						
FEB						
MAR	0	0	0	0	0	0
APR	1	1	1	1	1	1
MAY	2	2	2	2	2	2
JUN	3	3	3	3	3	3
JUL		4	4	4	4	4
AUG		5	5	5	5	5
SEP		6	6	6	6	6
OCT		7	7	7	7	7
NOV		8	8	8	8	8
DEC		9	9	9	9	9

The Princeton Review

4. SEX

MALE

FEMALE

Practice Test 2

1. A B C D
2. F G H J
3. A B C D
4. F G H J
5. A B C D
6. F G H J
7. A B C D
8. F G H J
9. A B C D
10. F G H J
11. A B C D
12. F G H J
13. A B C D
14. F G H J
15. A B C D
16. F G H J
17. A B C D
18. F G H J
19. A B C D
20. F G H J
21. A B C D
22. F G H J
23. A B C D
24. F G H J
25. A B C D
26. F G H J
27. A B C D
28. F G H J
29. A B C D
30. F G H J
31. A B C D
32. F G H J
33. A B C D
34. F G H J
35. A B C D

PRACTICE VIRGINIA SOL READING TEST 2

Sharing

Every game is better
when someone else is there.
Doing things together
shows someone that you care.
Everyone is happier
when you decide to share.

Toys that once were lonely
can now come out and play.
The weather doesn't matter
even on a rainy day.
Boredom doesn't stand a chance,
sharing chases it away.

Hiking is more special
when two people see a sight.
Watching scary movies with a friend,
means the darkness has a light.
Everything's more fun together.
That's why sharing is so right.

Sharing makes you happy
when you are feeling blue.
Sharing books and cookies,
I share my poem with you.
Sharing can't be done alone.
That's why it needs you too.

Go to next page

1 **Here is a line from the poem.**

> **That's why sharing is so <u>right</u>.**

What word below rhymes with <u>right</u>?

A seat

B bite

C caught

D high

2 **Which line in the poem tells about THINGS?**

F 8

G 18

H 21

J 23

3 **Which line from the poem BEST describes the poem's main idea?**

A Toys that once were lonely can now come out and play.

B Every game is better when someone else is there.

C The weather doesn't matter even on a rainy day.

D Everything's more fun together. That's why sharing is so right.

4 **If the four words below were in alphabetical order, which word would come first?**

F toys

G movies

H friend

J sharing

5 **What do you think the narrator of this poem would most likely do?**

A ask someone for money

B steal a book from a friend's house

C give some ice cream to a friend

D stay home alone to play with a new toy

6 **Which line in the poem has a word at the end that rhymes with the last word of line 2?**

F 1

G 3

H 4

J 5

Go to next page

7 **Look at the picture below.**

What line from the poem is pictured above?

A Hiking is more special when two people see a sight.

B Every game is better when someone else is there.

C Watching scary movies with a friend means the darkness has a light.

D Sharing books and cookies, I share my poem with you.

8 **Look at this line from the poem.**

Boredom <u>doesn't</u> stand a chance, sharing chases it away.

Another way to write <u>doesn't</u> is —

F did not

G do not

H will not

J does not

9 **What lesson does this poem teach its readers?**

A Toys can get lonely.

B Rainy weather is scary.

C Sharing is a good thing.

D Hiking is a lot of fun.

Go to next page

Peaches Has an Adventure

1 There once was a dog named Peaches. For many years the most exciting thing Peaches ever did was play with her master. Each day her master would come into the backyard and throw the ball for her. Then one day something different happened.

2 Peaches was playing in the backyard, chewing on a bone. "Hey Peaches!" she heard a voice yell. She looked up and saw Willow, the dog from the next house over. Willow was peeking through the fence. She looked very excited. Peaches walked over to the fence and sat down.

3 "You have to come with me!" cried Willow. "I have found something amazing!"

4 Peaches ran to the back of the yard and wiggled under the fence. She met Willow by the edge of the woods. Together they ran quickly down a path that led deep into the woods. The two dogs ran for several minutes. Peaches had never been this far into the woods before. She knew her master would be mad if he found out. By the time Willow stopped, Peaches was out of breath.

5 "What is so important?" asked Peaches with her tongue hanging out. She wanted to get home as soon as she could.

6 "Look!" said Willow, pointing with her paw. Peaches could not believe her eyes. It was the biggest bone she had ever seen! It was even longer than her master's car! "I found this bone sticking out of the ground," said Willow. "It took a whole week to dig up. It is too big to chew and it tastes like a rock. I think that it has been buried for a long time."

7 Peaches thought for a while and then had an idea. "We must get our masters. If this is really a bone, our masters need to be warned that there are giant monsters living in these woods."

8 Willow agreed with this idea. The two dogs ran back home. They each barked and barked to get their masters' attention. Finally, they convinced their masters to follow them back to the woods. When Peaches' master saw the giant bone, he stopped and stared.

9 "Look at that!" he said to Willow's master. "We must call the museum's dinosaur professor. He will want to dig up the whole skeleton. Peaches and Willow, you are very good dogs. Now you are going to be <u>famous</u> around the world!"

Go to next page

10 In this story what is the meaning of the word <u>famous</u> in paragraph 9?

F well-known

G in trouble

H sent home

J hungry

11 Which list below of words from the story has been put in alphabetical order?

A Peaches, master, dinosaur, yard

B master, dinosaur, Peaches, yard

C yard, Peaches, dinosaur, master

D dinosaur, master, Peaches, yard

12 Which answer BEST describes what kind of story this is?

F tall tale

G biography

H ghost story

J true story

13 Peaches can be BEST described as —

A afraid

B unhappy

C serious

D lazy

14 What do you think Peaches's master learned in this story?

F He should stay out of the woods.

G He should listen to his dog.

H He should spend time at the museum.

J He should be afraid of dinosaurs.

Go to next page

15 **Look at this sentence from the story.**

It took a whole <u>week</u> to dig it up.

Which word has a middle part that sounds like <u>week</u>?

A break

B shell

C leak

D fine

16 **Where would be the BEST place for Peaches's master to find more information on dinosaurs?**

F a dictionary

G an encyclopedia

H a map

J a thesaurus

17 **Look at the time line below.**

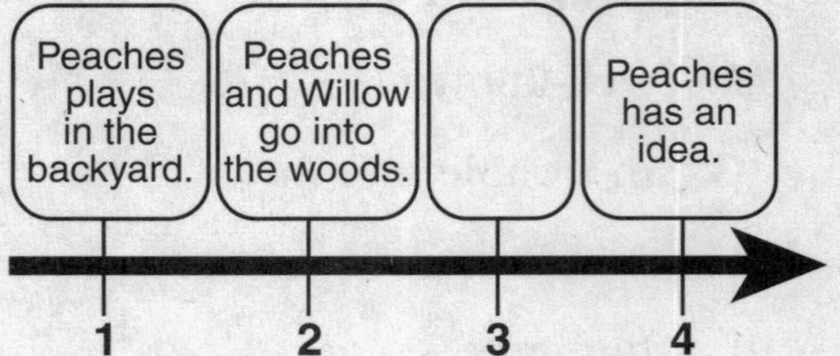

Which of these answers belongs in the third box?

A Peaches sees the bone.

B Peaches gets her master.

C Peaches chews on a bone.

D Peaches becomes famous.

18 **Peaches wants to show her master the bone because she —**

F thinks he will like it

G needs help carrying it

H thinks it is from a monster

J wants to become famous

Go to next page

Forest Friends

1 Jack loved camping with his brothers, Fred and Ralph. It was something they did every summer. Jack's favorite part was after dinner. The boys would roast marshmallows and tell stories. While he was telling a story, Jack noticed his brothers singing strange noises.

2 "Why are you doing that?" he asked them.

3 "To keep the animals happy," said Fred. "Otherwise, they won't bring us any berries for breakfast tomorrow morning."

4 "That's silly!" laughed Jack. "Animals don't bring people food."

5 "You're wrong," said Ralph. "In these woods the animals are special. If they like you, they bring you gifts at night. We sing to the animals because the animals like it. In return, they find the juiciest berries in the woods for us."

6 "You're making that up," said Jack. "Animals are not like that."

7 "If you don't believe us, then don't sing for them. But remember, they are watching you right now." Jack decided not to sing aloud.

8 Before going to bed, Fred and Ralph each put a pot on the ground. Jack saw this and put one out too.

9 The next morning Jack woke up first. When he opened the tent, he saw that two of the pots had big piles of blackberries in them, but his pot was empty. He woke his brothers up and said, "Hey! That wasn't funny. How come you got berries and I didn't?"

10 Fred said, "We told you. The animals leave the berries. You didn't sing to them."

11 Jack told them that he didn't think the joke was funny. All day he waited for his brothers to say that it was just a joke. However, neither one of them said anything. That night Fred and Ralph again sang loudly into the woods. This time they even yodeled.

12 "Why are you yodeling?" asked Jack.

13 "Because the animals like yodeling too," answered Ralph. Jack still thought they were playing a joke on him, but he decided to go along with it. He faced the woods and yodeled loudly. Once again, all three boys put pots next to the tent.

14 That night Jack tried to stay awake. He wanted to see if his brothers went berry picking. As hard as he tried, he still fell asleep. In the morning his brothers woke him up. "Wake up, sleepyhead!" yelled Ralph. "There are fresh berries for everyone."

15 Jack ran out of the tent. He saw that all three pots had handfuls of blackberries in them. Jack sighed. His brothers were going to tease him all the way home.

Go to next page

19 Look at the following picture.

Which word from the story has the same end sound as the word for what is shown in the picture above?

A berries

B ground

C Jack

D camp

20 Here is a sentence from the story.

> **"<u>You're</u> making that up," said Jack.**

Which answer shows another way of writing <u>You're</u>?

F You is

G You am

H You be

J You are

21 Why does Jack sing to the animals?

A He does not want to make the animals angry.

B He believes whatever his brothers tell him.

C He wants berries for breakfast.

D He does not like the taste of berries.

22 Look at the picture below.

What sentence from the story best describes this picture?

F The boys would roast marshmallows and tell stories.

G Hey! That wasn't funny. How come you got berries and I didn't?

H There are fresh berries for everyone.

J He faced the woods and yodeled loudly.

Go to next page

23 Why does Jack think his brothers are playing a joke on him?

A He knows that animals do not pick berries for people.

B His brothers are always playing mean tricks on him.

C It is something they always do while they roast marshmallows.

D He hears them talking and laughing after dinner.

24 Look at the sentence below.

All day he waited for them to say that it was just a <u>joke</u>.

Which of the following words rhymes with <u>joke</u>?

F pike

G smoke

H toy

J junk

25 What were Jack's brothers doing while he was telling his story?

A eating fresh berries

B setting up the tent

C cooking dinner

D singing strange noises

26 What is the lesson that Jack learns in this story?

F He really likes eating berries.

G His brothers can play good jokes.

H The best part about camping is telling stories.

J You can get berries from animals if you sing to them.

27 The next time the boys go camping, Jack will probably —

A steal the berries from his two brothers

B stay awake to see if his brothers pick the berries

C stay home because he is mad at his brothers

D eat by himself so that no one laughs at him

Go to next page

All Those Insects

1 Almost everyone has seen an insect. In fact, we see them all the time. But what do we really know about these little animals?

2 Insects are a very large group of animals. They have been on the Earth for millions of years. There are more than 800,000 kinds of insects that scientists know about. Plus there are probably many more kinds of insects that scientists haven't discovered yet!

3 Insects come in many shapes and sizes. Some insects are so small that you need a microscope to see them. Others are larger than your hand. An insect called a walkingstick can grow to be more than 12 inches long. Some butterflies and moths have wings almost that large. Many beetles grow to be 4 inches long.

4 Insects live almost everywhere on Earth. They live under the ground and in the water. They live in the trees. They even live in your house!

5 Insects eat many different kinds of food. For example, some grasshoppers eat leaves and grass. So do some beetles and ants. Termites and some ants eat wood. The young of many insects damage forests by eating all the leaves from the trees. Lots of insects are hunters. Like tiny lions, some ants, beetles, and wasps hunt other insects for food. Some insects bite people. Almost everyone has been bitten by a mosquito!

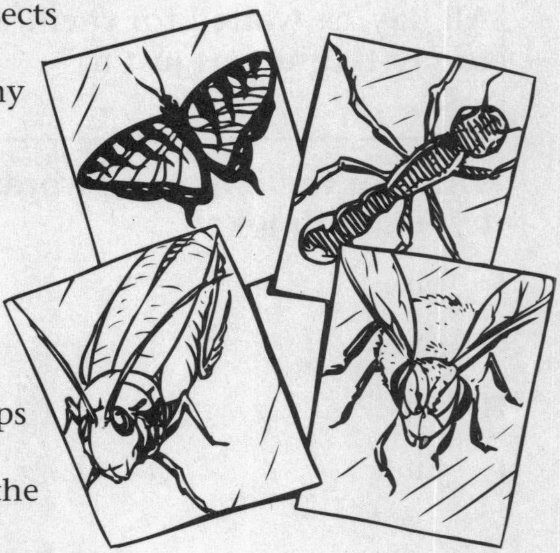

6 The most <u>remarkable</u> insects are the social insects. Social insects include bees, wasps, ants, and termites. We call them social insects because they live in large groups called hives. Each member of the hive has a job to do. Some hunt for food, some repair the nest, and some are guards. Each hive has a queen. The queen has a special job. She lays eggs. Hives can be very small or very large. Some hornet and wasp hives have only a few members. However, certain ant hives and beehives can have thousands of insects! Some termite hives in Africa are taller than a person!

7 Scientists learn something new about insects every day. With so many to study, that is not a surprise!

Go to next page

28 Read this line from paragraph 2.

> **Plus there are probably many more kinds of insects that scientists <u>haven't</u> discovered yet.**

What is another way of writing <u>haven't</u>?

F will not

G is not

H are not

J have not

29 Look at the picture below.

Which of the words from the story rhymes with the word for the item shown in this picture?

A ground

B four

C foot

D long

30 Look at the sentence below.

> **Some insects eat _____, while others do _____.**

Which words make this sentence complete and correct?

F wood, not

G would, not

H wood, knot

J would, knot

31 In paragraph 6 what does the word <u>remarkable</u> mean?

A friendly

B large

C hidden

D amazing

32 Scientists probably will be learning about insects for a long time because —

F there are so many insects to study

G insects eat many kinds of foods

H insects do not live at the South Pole

J many insects live in hives

Go to next page

33 **To find out more information on insects, the BEST thing to use would be —**

A a dictionary

B an encyclopedia

C a newspaper

D an atlas

34 **Which list below shows four words from the story listed in alphabetical order?**

F hives, insects, lions, grasshoppers

G lions, grasshoppers, insects, hives

H grasshoppers, hives, insects, lions

J insects, hives, lions, grasshoppers

35 **What insects sometimes build hives taller than a person?**

A termites

B beetles

C bees

D wasps

Completely darken bubbles with a No. 2 pencil. If you make a mistake, be sure to erase mark completely. Erase all stray marks.

1. YOUR NAME: ______ (Print) Last First M.I.

SIGNATURE: ______ DATE: / /

HOME ADDRESS: (Print) ______ Number

______ City State Zip Code

PHONE NO.: (Print) ______

2. YOUR NAME

First 4 letters of last name				FIRST INIT	MID INIT
A	A	A	A	A	A
B	B	B	B	B	B
C	C	C	C	C	C
D	D	D	D	D	D
E	E	E	E	E	E
F	F	F	F	F	F
G	G	G	G	G	G
H	H	H	H	H	H
I	I	I	I	I	I
J	J	J	J	J	J
K	K	K	K	K	K
L	L	L	L	L	L
M	M	M	M	M	M
N	N	N	N	N	N
O	O	O	O	O	O
P	P	P	P	P	P
Q	Q	Q	Q	Q	Q
R	R	R	R	R	R
S	S	S	S	S	S
T	T	T	T	T	T
U	U	U	U	U	U
V	V	V	V	V	V
W	W	W	W	W	W
X	X	X	X	X	X
Y	Y	Y	Y	Y	Y
Z	Z	Z	Z	Z	Z

3. DATE OF BIRTH

Month	Day		Year			
JAN						
FEB						
MAR	0	0	0	0	0	0
APR	1	1	1	1	1	1
MAY	2	2	2	2	2	2
JUN	3	3	3	3	3	3
JUL		4	4	4	4	4
AUG		5	5	5	5	5
SEP		6	6	6	6	6
OCT		7	7	7	7	7
NOV		8	8	8	8	8
DEC		9	9	9	9	9

The Princeton Review

4. SEX

MALE

FEMALE

Practice Test 3

1. A B C D	8. F G H J	15. A B C D	22. F G H J	29. A B C D
2. F G H J	9. A B C D	16. F G H J	23. A B C D	30. F G H J
3. A B C D	10. F G H J	17. A B C D	24. F G H J	31. A B C D
4. F G H J	11. A B C D	18. F G H J	25. A B C D	32. F G H J
5. A B C D	12. F G H J	19. A B C D	26. F G H J	33. A B C D
6. F G H J	13. A B C D	20. F G H J	27. A B C D	34. F G H J
7. A B C D	14. F G H J	21. A B C D	28. F G H J	35. A B C D

PRACTICE VIRGINIA SOL READING TEST 3

A Walk in the Park

1 Kevin O'Shea opened his door and got out of the car. Kevin's dog, Sparky, jumped out after him. Sparky started running and jumping right away. "Don't let Sparky run too far away," said Mr. O'Shea.

2 "I won't, Dad," replied Kevin. "I really love Dog Park. Isn't it great that the town allows dogs to run loose in this park?"

3 Mr. O'Shea smiled and nodded. He looked around at the big field that made up the center of the park. Everywhere he looked, he saw dogs walking, running, and playing catch. Dog Park was the newest park in town. Ever since it opened, it had become very popular. It was the only place in town where dogs did not have to wear leashes. People brought their dogs to the park to get exercise and play with other dogs.

4 Kevin and his dad walked down the path that led to the big field. They saw dogs fetching sticks and chasing each other. Kevin threw a ball for Sparky. Sparky would chase the ball and bring it back. Sparky loved coming to the park. As they walked, Kevin and Mr. O'Shea met other people with dogs. Sparky and the other dogs played together, running back and forth. Mr. O'Shea talked with the other owners. Kevin threw the ball for the dogs.

5 After an hour Mr. O'Shea noticed that the sun was going down. "Kevin, it is starting to get dark. You should turn on Sparky's collar." Kevin pushed a button on Sparky's collar. A row of red lights came on and started blinking. The lights were so bright that Kevin could see them even if Sparky was across the field.

6 "Where did you get that collar?" someone asked Mr. O'Shea.

7 "I made it myself," said Mr. O'Shea. "Sparky has black fur, and we couldn't see him at night. We needed a collar with lights on it. None of the stores around had one, so I made one. I used a battery and some old holiday lights." All of the people who saw Sparky that night agreed that Mr. O'Shea's collar was the best idea they had ever seen. Several people ever asked Kevin's father to make collars for their dogs!

Go to next page

1 **Look at the sentence below.**

Isn't it great that the town allows dogs to run <u>loose</u> in this park?"

What word rhymes with <u>loose</u>?

A push

B boss

C goose

D choice

2 **What lesson does Kevin learn in the story?**

F Kevin's father has made a useful invention.

G Collars are not helpful when it gets dark outside.

H Sparky and the other dogs played together.

J It is hard to find a nice place to play catch with your dog.

3 **What makes Dog Park so special?**

A It is the oldest park in town.

B All dogs wear special collars there.

C Mr. O'Shea helped to build it.

D Dogs do not need leashes there.

4 **Look at the picture below.**

Which word begins with the same sound as the word illustrated in the picture?

F chop

G shoe

H collar

J know

5 **How did Mr. O'Shea solve the problem of not being able to see Sparky at night?**

A He made a collar with lights.

B He kept Sparky on a leash.

C He let other people walk Sparky.

D He only walked Sparky during the day.

Go to next page

6 **Look at the sentence from the story.**

> **Sparky has black fur, and we <u>couldn't</u> see him at night.**

Which pair of words shows a different way to write <u>couldn't</u>?

F could not

G will not

H does not

J am not

7 **Look at the picture below.**

Which part of the story does this picture illustrate?

A Dog Park was the newest park in town.

B Kevin's dog, Sparky, jumped out after him.

C As they walked, Kevin and Mr. O'Shea met other people with dogs.

D Sparky would chase the ball and bring it back.

8 **The other people in the Dog Park will probably —**

F start walking in another park

G tell Kevin to put Sparky on a leash

H ask Mr. O'Shea to make more collars

J help Mr. O'Shea build a better park

9 **What did Mr. O'Shea tell Kevin to do when it started to get dark?**

A turn on Sparky's collar

B watch other people walking their dogs

C keep Sparky close by

D notice how nice the park was

Go to next page

Across the Sky

High, high above the clouds,
so high above the ground.
Soaring o'er the Earth they are,
from there it looks so round.

Too high to see our faces,
to them we are just dots.
Moving across the sky so fast,
while we stay in one spot.

With steel wings and engines loud
the planes fly through the air.
Carrying people, many people,
from where to who knows where.

The pilots fly the planes so well
through night and through the day.
The crews make sure the planes runs right,
and safe and sound they stay.

Down here I look into the sky
and watch planes go to and fro.
And every time I see one pass
I wonder, where does it go?

Go to next page

10 Here is a line from "Across the Sky."

> **With steel wings and engines <u>loud</u>**

What word below rhymes with <u>loud</u>?

F floor

G power

H frog

J proud

11 Which list below shows four words from the poem in alphabetical order?

A faces, Earth, sky, pilot

B Earth, pilot, sky, faces

C Earth, faces, pilot, sky

D pilot, faces, Earth, sky

12 Which line in the poem talks about a person doing an ACTION?

F 6

G 10

H 14

J 18

13 What do you think the narrator of this poem would most likely do?

A ride on a train

B read a book about airplanes

C play with a model car

D stay inside and bake cookies

14 Look at the picture below.

What line from the poem is pictured above?

F Carrying people, many people

G High, high above the clouds

H The pilots fly the planes so well

J With steel wings and engines loud

Go to next page

15 Look at this sentence from the poem.

> **Too high to see our faces, to them <u>we are</u> just dots.**

A different way to write <u>we are</u> is —

A he'll

B wasn't

C there'll

D we're

16 Which line in the poem has a word at the end that rhymes with the word at end of line 14?

F 13

G 15

H 16

J 18

17 In this poem what is the narrator doing?

A flying in a plane

B watching airplanes

C watching a movie

D going on an adventure

18 What question do lines 13 though 16 answer?

F What do the passengers on an airplane do?

G Where are the people in the airplane going?

H How high does an airplane fly?

J What do the pilot and crew of an airplane do?

Go to next page

Ally's Race

1 Faster and faster she went down the hill. The people rushed by so quickly that they seemed like a blur. Ally's eyes watered as the wind blew into her face. She gripped the wheel as tightly as she could. She wondered if entering the go-cart race had been a good idea. She had never gone so fast in her life! Around her the other cars moved back and forth, trying to get ahead of each other. Ally was so scared that she couldn't think about passing anyone. All she could focus on was staying straight and not hitting anything.

2 Beneath her she could feel the wooden go-cart shake. Every bump in the road felt ten times bigger than it actually was. As she passed the halfway marker, she felt as if the race had already been going on forever. Now she could see the finish line up ahead. It grew steadily larger. The wind roared like a lion in her ears, and she couldn't hear anything else. Inside her helmet she was sweating with fear. She was afraid that someone would hit her cart. She was afraid that she would miss the brake with her foot and crash. She was afraid of a hundred things.

3 Suddenly, the finish line flashed by her and she remembered to step on the brake. Slowly, the car came to a stop. Around her the other cars were stopping too. A crowd of people ran to the carts. The other drivers started getting out of their carts. Ally just sat there. Her legs felt like noodles. She didn't think they would hold her if she stood up.

4 Her parents ran up to her cart. "Congratulations!" they screamed. "You came in third place!"

5 Ally sat there, trying to believe what she had heard. Third place? Suddenly all her fear went away. She jumped out of the cart and hugged her parents. "That was so much fun!" she said. "I can't wait to race again next week!"

Go to next page

19 **Which sentence from the story tells what Ally has learned?**

A Ally was so scared that she couldn't think about passing anyone.

B "I can't wait to race again next week!"

C A crowd of people ran to the carts.

D She didn't think they would hold her if she stood up.

20 **Look at this sentence from paragraph 1.**

> **She <u>gripped</u> the wheel as tightly as she could.**

The word <u>gripped</u> in this sentence means —

F held on to

G threw away

H tried to hide

J thought about

21 **What word from the story has the same middle vowel sound as <u>snake</u>?**

A faster

B all

C ahead

D race

22 **What word BEST describes how Ally feels after the race is over?**

F excited

G afraid

H bored

J tired

23 **What was Ally afraid of doing?**

A losing the race

B seeing her parents

C stepping on the brake

D hitting another go-cart

24 **What makes Ally change her mind about entering the next race?**

F She is upset that she has lost the race.

G Her parents tell her that she has to enter it.

H She finishes the race in third place.

J Her legs feel like noodles.

Go to next page

25 Look at the picture below.

Which sentence from the story does the picture show?

A Every bump in the road felt ten times bigger than it actually was.

B Suddenly, the finish line flashed by her and she remembered to step on the brake.

C She didn't think they would hold her if she stood up.

D She jumped out of the cart and hugged her parents.

26 Look at the time line below.

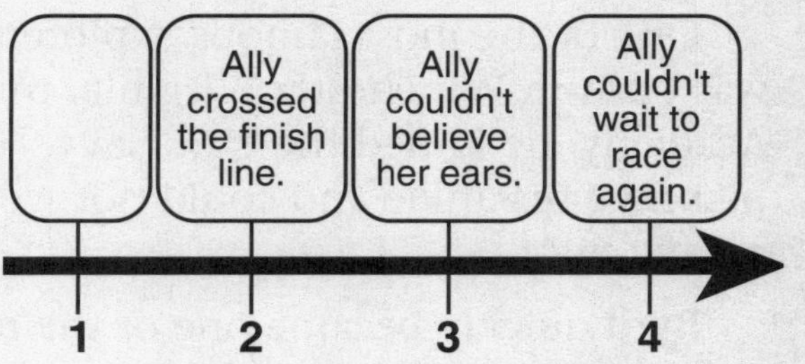

Which answer belongs in space 1 of the time line?

F Ally's eyes watered from the wind.

G Ally's parents congratulated her.

H Ally came in third place.

J Ally's legs felt like noodles.

27 Before she finishes the race, Ally feels —

A ready to pass as many go-carts as she can

B frightened because she is going so fast

C eager to enter another go-cart race

D excited to be winning the race

Go to next page

From Virginia to the South Pole

1 One of the most famous explorers to have lived is Admiral Richard Byrd. He was born in Winchester, Virginia, in 1888. After graduating from the U.S. Naval Academy, he joined the U.S. Navy. He served on a battleship until 1916, when he broke his ankle and could not work on a ship anymore. In 1918 he became a navy pilot.

2 Byrd quickly became one of the most <u>skilled</u> pilots in the navy. He invented a way to land planes on the ocean at night. He was also very good at flying far out over the ocean. Even when he could not see any land, he could always find his way back to shore.

3 For his entire life, Admiral Richard Byrd had always wanted to explore the North Pole. In 1926 he planned a trip to the North Pole. Byrd and another pilot, Floyd Bennett, flew a plane over the North Pole. On May 9, 1926, they became the first people to ever reach the North Pole by plane. Both pilots were awarded the Medal of Honor when they returned to the United States. Byrd became a hero.

4 Byrd was not satisfied to explore only the North Pole. Byrd also wanted to go to the South Pole. The South Pole is even colder than the North Pole! On November 29, 1929, Byrd and three of his companions became the first people to fly over the South Pole. In 1934 he traveled to the South Pole again. He spent the winter living in a hut near the South Pole. Storms would last for days, and he almost died. After this second trip Byrd rejoined the navy. He made three more trips to the South Pole before he died in 1957.

Go to next page

28 Look at the drawing of a number.

What word from the story ends with the same sound as the name of the number shown above?

F explore

G people

H born

J work

29 Read the two sentences below about Admiral Byrd.

Admiral Byrd _____ a plane in the Navy. He was good at landing planes at _____.

Which two words correctly fills in the blanks?

A flew, see

B flu, sea

C flew, sea

D flu, see

30 What would be the BEST place to find more information about Admiral Byrd?

F a dictionary

G an atlas

H a map

J a biography

31 If Admiral Byrd had lived longer, he probably would have —

A gone back to being a sailor

B continued doing research on the South Pole

C become afraid to fly in a plane

D decided not to explore anymore

Go to next page

32 **Look at the sentence from the story.**

> **In 1916 he broke his ankle and <u>could not</u> work on a ship anymore.**

What is another way of writing <u>could not</u>?

F can't

G couldn't

H didn't

J doesn't

33 **In paragraph 2 what does the word <u>skilled</u> mean?**

A brand new

B old

C friendly

D talented

34 **Based on this story which pair of words BEST describes Admiral Byrd?**

F frightened and nervous

G lazy and silly

H determined and daring

J angry and serious

35 **What did Admiral Byrd do after he flew over the North Pole?**

A He worked on a navy ship.

B He broke his ankle.

C He explored the South Pole.

D He learned how to land planes on the water.

Answers to Miles and Map Checks

Mile 1: Word Sounds

1. Lunch
2. Phone
3. Garden
4. How
5. Shadow
6 House
7. Keep
8. Sugar
9. Sing
10. Cloud
11. Strange
12. Zero
13. Stole
14. Luck
15. Drink
16. Move
17. Sand
18. Team
19. High
20. Mess
21. Own
22. Fire

Mile 2: Rhyme

1. 4
2. 12
3. 16
4. Toe
5. Call
6. Fun
7. Dove

There are many right answers for questions 8, 9, and 10. Here are some examples.

8. Tool
9. Rat
10. Charm

Mile 3: Homophones

1. *tale*
2. *sea*
3. *bee*
4. *some*
5. *would*
6. *Blue*
7. *Two*
8. *Do*
9. *Choose*
10. *Eye*
11. knew heard there buy hour
12. would made whole seen week

Map Check 1

1. C
2. J
3. C
4. H
5. A
6. H
7. B
8. F
9. D
10. F
11. C
12. J
13. A
14. J
15. C
16. H
17. A

Mile 5: Nouns, Verbs, Adjectives, and Adverbs

1. verb
2. adverb
3. noun
4. noun
5. verb
6. adverb
7. adjective
8. noun
9. adjective
10. noun
11. adjective
12. verb
13. noun
14. adjective
15. noun
16. verb
17. adverb
18. adjective
19. noun
20. adjective
21. noun
22. adjective
23. adjective
24. noun
25. adjective
26. noun
27. adjective
28. adjective
29. noun
30. verb
31. adverb
32. verb
33. adjective
34. noun
35. noun
36. adjective
37. adjective
38. adjective
39. noun
40. verb
41. adjective
42. noun
43. verb
44. adverb
45. adjective
46. noun

Mile 6: Prefixes and Suffixes

Diego stared in disbelief at the dinosaur. It roared loudly and walked toward him. Along the way, it crushed an unlucky bush with its large feet. As it got closer, Diego saw that the dinosaur's left arm was incomplete, missing its hand. Just then the dinosaur stopped moving. A woman walked over to the dinosaur. She undid a panel on the dinosaur's shin and fixed a loose wire. Then she shut the panel. She then hit a button on a remote control to restart the dinosaur. The dinosaur started moving again. Soon the museum's new display would be complete.

Michelle looked into the living room. Her dog, Fredo, was asleep on the couch. He looked so peaceful. She decided to take a picture of him. She got her camera out of the closet, but the film had no pictures left. Michelle wished that someone would invent reusable film. She sat down to watch a television show about art. A painter was teaching people about colors. Michelle had tried to paint in art class, but she thought she was hopeless. She quickly changed the channel to something she liked better.

Mile 7: Contractions

1. should not
2. could not
3. could have
4. did not
5. should have
6. we will
7. they will
8. It is
9. I am
10. I have
11. Where's
12. She's
13. He's
14. aren't
15. don't
16. it's
17. I'd
18. he'd
19. wouldn't
20. he'll
21. he'd
22. he'll

Mile 8: Abbreviations

1. Tuesday
2. Mister
3. Street
4. Reverend
5. September
6. Thursday
7. Wednesday
8. January
9. Doctor
10. Friday
11. Monday
12. Avenue
13. February
14. Saturday

Mile 9: Who Owns It?

1. Mary's
2. brother's
3. Daddy's
4. Mia's
5. ocean's
6. movie's
7. snake's
8. Mike's
9. train's
10. Harvey's
11. cat's
12. pen's
13. phone's
14. shirt's
15. Sheila's

Map Check 2

1. A
2. H
3. B
4. J
5. D
6. G
7. A
8. G
9. D
10. H
11. B
12. J
13. C
14. F
15. C

Mile 10: Before Reading Stories

1. *An adventure about a puppy*
2. *Information about insects*
3. *A mystery about a stolen statue*
4. *Recipes for cooking meals*
5. *Lessons on how to drive a car*
6. *A road map of Virginia*
7. *Lessons on how to use the Internet*
8. *Information about Babe Ruth*

Mile 11: Fiction or Nonfiction?

A. *Fiction*

B. *Nonfiction*

1. *Nonfiction*
2. *Fiction*
3. *Fiction*
4. *Nonfiction*
5. *Nonfiction*
6. *Fiction*
7. *Nonfiction*
8. *Fiction*
9. *Fiction*
10. *Nonfiction*
11. *Nonfiction*
12. *Fiction*
13. *Fiction*
14. *Nonfiction*
15. *Nonfiction*

There are many right answers for a fiction or nonfiction sentence. Here are two examples.

Fiction: Doug and Sally liked to play in the tall waves.

Nonfiction: Dolphins breathe through holes on the tops of their heads.

Mile 12: Why Do People Read?

Remember that different people read for different reasons. So your answers may be different and also right!

To have fun	To gain knowledge	To learn how to do things
Fairy tales	Autobiographies	Recipes
Plays	Maps	Art Projects
Poems	Newspaper Articles	Science Experiments
Myths	Magazine Articles	Directions
Humorous Stories	Encyclopedia Articles	
	Schedules	
	Scientific Illustrations	
	Weather Reports	
	Dictionary Definitions	
	History Textbooks	

1. a dictionary *Somebody might read this selection to find out the meaning of a word.*
2. a recipe *Somebody might read this selection to learn how to cook something.*
3. an encyclopedia article *Somebody might read this selection to learn about moose.*
4. a story *Somebody might read this selection to enjoy the story.*
5. a biography *Somebody might read this selection to learn about our first president.*
6. a poem *Somebody might read this selection for fun.*
7. a recipe *Somebody might read this selection to learn how to make a cake.*
8. a story *Somebody might read this selection to enjoy the story.*
9. a dictionary *Somebody might read this selection to learn what the word "cat" means.*
10. a poem *Somebody might read this selection for fun.*
11. a biography *Somebody might read this selection to learn about Babe Ruth.*

MILE 13: FINDING THE MAIN IDEA

1. *Jane Finds a Snake*
2. *Mike learns not to be afraid of snakes.*
3. *Reptiles*
4. *Snakes, lizards, turtles, and crocodiles are all reptiles. All reptiles shed their skin.*
5. *The Stranger*
6. *People were scared of the new stranger in town until they learned that she was the new pastor.*
7. *Cowboy Dress*
8. *There is a reason why cowboys dress the way that they do.*
9. *Chet Atkins learned to play the guitar when he was young. He wrote many famous songs for himself. Many famous guitar players say he was their role model. He kept making music until he died in 2001.*
10. *This is a biography about the life of a famous guitar player, Chet Atkins.*

MAP CHECK 3

1. A
2. G
3. D
4. G
5. D
6. H
7. D
8. F
9. D
10. G
11. D
12. H
13. B
14. J
15. B
16. F
17. D
18. J
19. A
20. H
21. A
22. G

MILE 14: FINDING SUPPORTING IDEAS

We have filled in the graphic organizer below with some examples. Any fact from the passage is a correct answer.

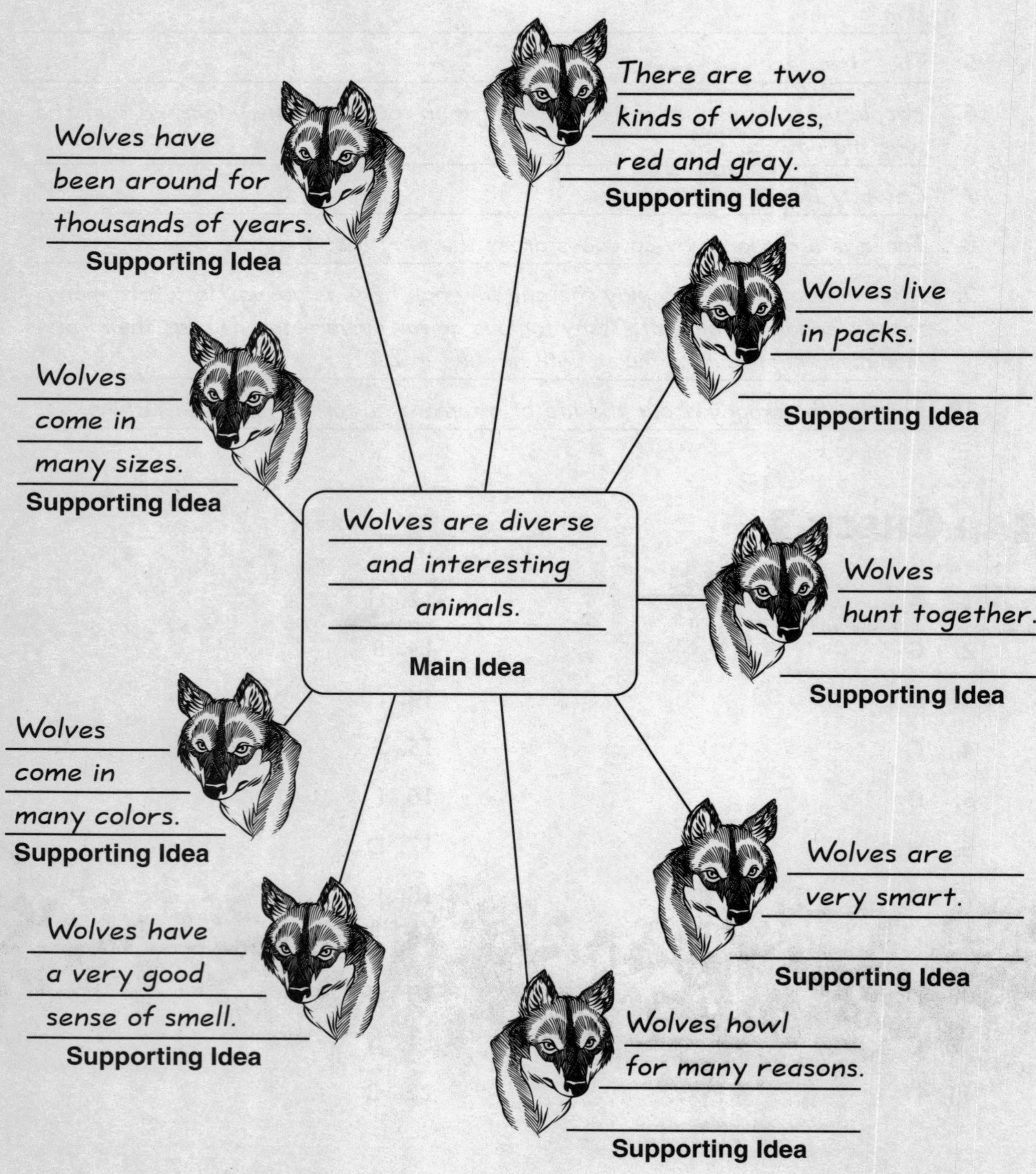

Wolves are diverse and interesting animals.
Main Idea
There are two kinds of wolves, red and gray.
Supporting Idea
Wolves live in packs.
Supporting Idea
Wolves hunt together.
Supporting Idea
Wolves are very smart.
Supporting Idea
Wolves howl for many reasons.
Supporting Idea
Wolves have a very good sense of smell.
Supporting Idea
Wolves come in many colors.
Supporting Idea
Wolves come in many sizes.
Supporting Idea
Wolves have been around for thousands of years.
Supporting Idea

Mile 15: Answering Questions About Details

1. *Officer Clarke knew that the burglar broke into the store through the window because the broken glass was on the inside of the store.*
2. *The hole in the floor went into a tunnel.*
3. *Solving a crime is like putting together a puzzle.*
4. *Real detectives spend more time looking for clues than they do chasing bad guys.*
5. *The diver is looking for treasure.*
6. *The diver doesn't float because he is wearing heavy boots.*
7. *One of the dangers was having a leaky suit. (They also had to worry about getting an air hose caught on a rock.)*
8. *Today divers carry their air in special tanks.*

Mile 16: Learning New Words

1. weak
2. hungry
3. group
4. save
5. rare

Mile 17: Drawing Conclusions

1. *The girl is not going to school because she is sick.*
2. *People are having a party because it is the boy's birthday.*
3. *The softball players are celebrating because the team has won the game.*
4. *The people are packing their bags because they're going away for vacation.*
5. *The girl and her grandfather are getting ready to go fishing.*
6. *Benny's tail was wagging because he was happy.*
7. *Benny began to shake because he was afraid of the bear.*
8. *The other animals might not want to be Benny's friend because they would be afraid that Benny would let the bear hurt them.*
9. *Fluffy was crying because he had no friends and was afraid Benny would not be his friend.*

Map Check 4

1. B
2. H
3. D
4. F
5. B
6. F
7. D
8. F
9. D
10. G
11. D
12. H
13. D
14. G
15. A
16. F
17. B
18. G
19. D
20. G

Mile 18: Characters, Settings, and Events

1.

Character	Adjective
Anika	happy
Anika's father	generous and nice
Mr. Foley	helpful

2. *The story mainly takes place in the store Anything You Want.*
3. *The story take places on a Saturday.*
4. *The main problem in the story is that the store Anika wants to buy her hat in is closed.*
5. *The main problem is solved when Anika finds a hat in a new store.*
6. *The lesson of this story is that you can find what you want if you look hard enough.*
7. *Olaf ties up the dogs*
8. *Olaf falls asleep*
9. *A wave hits the beach*
10. *The whale pushes Olaf to shore*

MILE 19: GETTING INSIDE A CHARACTER'S HEAD

1. *Ollie is unhappy because he has been there before.*

   The clue is that Ollie sighs when he hears where they are going.

2. *Stacy tells Ollie to be quiet because she is tired of his complaining and wants to learn.*

   The clue is that she frowns when she tells Ollie to be quiet.

3. *Ollie pays attention to Sue because he realizes that he is going to learn something new.*

   The clue is that Ollie is excited when Sue asks him if he wants to see where the food for the animals is made. He also tells Stacy that he learned something new.

Ollie

Upset over the trip to the zoo

Bored with learning about zoo animals

Surprised to learn something new about the zoo

Stacy

Interested in seeing the animals at the zoo

Angry with Ollie for complaining

Sue the Guide

Happy to show the children something new

MILE 20: MAKING PREDICTIONS

1. *I think Rhoda will tell everyone who stole the art supplies.*
2. *I think Rhoda will be a hero.*
3. *Who stole the paint and brushes from the classroom?*
4. *Rhoda did not tell everyone, just the principal.*
5. *Rhoda went to the principal's office instead of telling everyone in class the next day.*
6. *Rhoda tells the principal about the clues that she found, and the principal looks up the names of the students. Mr. Cole tells Rhoda that he is proud of her and that she saved art class.*
7. *It was very close, except that Rhoda only told the principal.*
8. *Rhoda may decide to become a detective.*
9. *Yes, my question was answered.*

MAP CHECK 5

1. C
2. F
3. B
4. H
5. A
6. J
7. B
8. H
9. A
10. H
11. A
12. G
13. D
14. H
15. C
16. J
17. C
18. F
19. D
20. F
21. B

MILE 21: ELEMENTS OF POETRY

1. *Mood*
2. *Theme*
3. *Rhyme*
4. *Rhythm*
5. *Stanza*
6. *4*
7. *1 and 2, 3 and 4*
8. *The frog feels joyful about his pond.*
9. *You know how the frog feels because it says the pond fulfills its every wish.*
10. *Happy*

Mile 22: Making Comparisons

1. *Both poems are about the summer. They share the same topic.*
2. *The theme of the second poem is different from the theme of the first because in the second poem, the narrator thinks summer goes by too quickly.*
3. *Fun*
4. *Excited*
5. *Summer days are like dreams.*
6. *Poem 2*
7. *Both*
8. *Poem 1*
9. *Poem 1*
10. *Poem 2*

Map Check 6

1. C
2. F
3. B
4. J
5. B
6. H
7. A
8. G
9. A
10. H
11. D
12. F
13. A
14. H
15. A
16. H
17. D
18. J
19. B
20. F
21. A

Mile 23: Alphabetizing

1. *Alice's Adventures in Wonderland*
2. *Babe: the Gallant Pig*
3. *Charlotte's Web*
4. *Harry Potter and the Sorcerer's Stone*
5. *James and the Giant Peach*
6. *Old Yeller*
7. *Sarah, Plain and Tall*
8. *Where the Sidewalk Ends*

1. Carroll, Lewis
2. Dahl, Roald
3. Gipson, Fred
4. King-Smith, Dick
5. MacLachlan, Patricia
6. Rowling, J. K.
7. Silverstein, Shel
8. White, E. B.

1.	Cow	Duck	Horse	Mouse	Turkey
2.	Alysha	Chuck	Moira	Richard	Tom
3.	Boston	Detroit	Houston	Miami	Reston
4.	Birch	Elm	Hickory	Maple	Oak
5.	Casper	Mittens	Rudy	Snowball	Whiskers

Mile 24: Using a Dictionary

1. *noun*
2. *deck*
3. *The definition of a word tells you its meaning.*
4. *dĕk*
5. *The siren on the police car was very loud.*
6. *The example sentence shows how to use the word in a sentence.*
7. *Gab means to talk a lot.*
8. *A dictionary shows the meanings of words. It tells you how to spell and pronounce words.*

MILE 25: USING A TABLE OF CONTENTS AND AN INDEX

1. The Forest Fire
2. Page 60
3. Chapter 10
4. Chapter 3
5. Page 44
6. 10
7. Page 12
8. 4-6
9. 0
10. Lasagna (or Pasta)

MILE 26: USING CHARTS

1. 7:00 A.M.
2. 8:15 A.M.
3. 129
4. 1

Schedule for Gopher Scouts Award Dinner

4:00 P.M. Auditorium doors open

4:30 P.M. All guests should be seated

4:45 P.M. Gopher Scoutmaster Wilson introduces the guest speakers

5:00 P.M. First guest speaker

5:15 P.M. Second guest speaker

5:30 P.M. Dinner is served

6:30 P.M. Dessert is served

7:00 P.M. Awards are announced

8:00 P.M. Award dinner is over

MILE 27: FINDING OUT MORE

1. *encyclopedia*
2. *dictionary*
3. *atlas*
4. *thesaurus*
5. *almanac or encyclopedia*
6. *library*
7. *encyclopedia*
8. *dictionary*
9. *atlas*
10. *thesaurus*
11. *almanac*
12. *library*
13. *dictionary*
14. *dictionary*
15. *encyclopedia*
16. *atlas*

MAP CHECK 7

1. C
2. G
3. D
4. F
5. A
6. H
7. D
8. J
9. C
10. F
11. C
12. G
13. B
14. F
15. B
16. F
17. B
18. H
19. C
20. J

Practice Test Answers and Explanations

Practice Test 1 Answers and Explanations

Guarding the Sheep

1 **B** Milo gets in trouble for not guarding the sheep. No bears are seen during the story, so **D** is not right. **A** and **C** are not good choices because not enough information is given for readers to know if they are true or not.

2 **F** A folktale is a tale that is fictional and teaches a lesson or moral. Animals don't really talk. But animals talk in this story, so it must be fiction. Plus, this story teaches a lesson. There are no ghosts, so **G** can't be true. It is not a history lesson, so **H** can't be true either.

3 **D** Read the sentence from the box. Say the word <u>know</u> to yourself. It ends with a long "o" sound. Now look at the answer choices. *Toe* is the only word with the long "o" sound at the end. None of the other words ends with an "o" sound.

4 **J** Sally does not send the other sheep away, she does not count them, and she does not lie to them. She gathers them around her to speak to them. That is what makes **J** the correct answer choice.

5 **A** Look at the answer choices carefully. Try to find the words that are in alphabetical order, based on the first letter of each word. If an answer choice lists the words out of order, it can't be correct. Only **A** lists all four words in correct alphabetical order.

6 **H** Sally is smart. She finds a way to keep the other sheep safe and teach the dog an important lesson. Because you know that Sally is not evil, dangerous, or tired, you can throw out answer choices **F, G,** and **J.**

7 **A** The main idea of this story is that a lazy dog learns a lesson. The ideas in **B** and **C** do happen in the story, but they are not what the whole story is about. The sheep do not learn any lessons about running away in the story. **A** is the best answer choice.

8 **J** Milo has learned a lesson in the story. Milo has learned not to sleep anymore while he is working. He will probably not fall asleep again, so **F** is incorrect. The farmer is not going to keep his watchdog in the barn, so **G** is incorrect. Since Milo says he has learned a lesson, he will probably not get Sally in trouble, so **H** is wrong too.

MAKING MONEY

9 B An encyclopedia is the best source to find more information about things. You can use a dictionary to look up the definitions of words. So **C** is not right in this case. A thesaurus lists words that have the same meaning as another word. So **A** is not right in this case. A biography tells about a person's life. So **D** is also not right.

10 H Follow the events in the time line. What happens between when "a die is made from a plastic model" and "coins are examined"? Does an artist make a plastic model of the coin? No, that happens *first*. Now you know **F** is wrong. Does a machine count the coins or are they sent to a bank? No, that happens *after* they are examined. So **G** and **J** are wrong too. **H** fits into the time line. The blank metal is stamped.

11 A The coins are looked at to make sure there is nothing wrong with them. The story does not talk about coins being played with or stolen, so **C** and **D** are not correct. The coins are counted, but that occurs later in the paragraph. If it helps, try putting the words in the answer choices into the real sentence. Only the right answer choice should sound right.

12 J J is correct. Both "kid" and "coins" begin with a hard "c" sound. "Change" and "chew" begin with a different sound, so they're not right. "Gold" begins with a "g" sound, so it's not right, either.

13 B It is hard to make a coin because there are many important and detailed steps to go through. Coins are not made in just one place. All coins do not look the same. Plus, coins are made of metal, not plastic. **B** makes the most sense.

14 J Fill in the words that complete the sentences in the box. Look for the correct words. "Cent" and "one" are the two words that are correct. "Scent" refers to smell, and "won" means winning something. Neither of those words makes sense in the sentences in the box.

15 A The first paragraph tells the places where coins are made. The questions asked in **B** and **C** are answered later in the story. Dollar bills are not part of this story, so **D** is wrong.

16 G The book listed in **G** is the right answer. It is the only book about making money, which is what is done at mints. The other books might mention coins, but would not tell about how they are made.

UNDERWATER PIONEER

17 C Read the sentence in the box. Look for the answer choice that means the same thing. **C** is correct. The important fact is that divers did not get air from the boats anymore. They still needed air to breathe, and they still needed to ride in boats to get to places.

18 F What is the picture of? It's a fish! Now look for a word that rhymes with "fish." Say it aloud if it helps. "Fish" rhymes with "wish." If you sound out "test," "push," and "list," you will find that they do not rhyme with fish.

19 C Look for the word <u>solve</u> in paragraph 3. Jacques Cousteau had to <u>solve</u> a problem. Try the answer choices. Does that mean he had to "question" a problem? That doesn't make sense. Did he have to "take a test about" a problem? No way. Did he have to "make" a problem? Nope. Did he have to "find the answer to" a problem? Yes, he did! **B** is the correct answer choice.

20 J Try to find the pair of words that fits the two sentences. Only one answer choice is correct. "See" means to look with your eyes, and a "maid" is a person who cleans. Only "sea" and "made" make sense in these sentences.

21 C The Cousteau Society probably still makes movies about the oceans. Since the Cousteau Society made movies when Cousteau was alive, it makes sense that it would continue to do this. It wouldn't take people on long fishing trips or sell boats!

22 G Jacques Cousteau can be BEST described as daring, brave, and curious. He was daring because he did things no one had ever done before. He was brave because some of the things he did were dangerous. He was curious because he liked to learn about new things.

23 A To find out more information about scuba divers, the BEST source to look in would be an encyclopedia. An encyclopedia is where you look up information about different subjects. You would use a dictionary to find out the definition of the word "scuba." Scuba divers would probably not be mentioned in a math book or an atlas.

24 H This question asks what the *last* problem Cousteau had to solve was. He had to learn how to swim with fins on and be able to see underwater *first*. The Cousteau Society came much later. **H** is the best answer choice.

25 B The "Underwater Pioneer" is a biography. That makes **B** correct. A biography tells about someone's life. A fairytale or a fable is a story that is not true. It is also not a poem.

Finally Spring

26 F F is the correct choice because "kite" and "might" rhyme with each other. "Crate," "bit," and "seat" all have different sounds at their ends.

27 D Read line 4 from the poem. Now look for the line that ends with a word that rhymes with spring. "With gifts to share and bring" ends with a word that rhymes with "spring." That's line 6. None of the other three lines in the answer choices ends in a word that rhymes with "spring."

28 H Read the lists to find words from the poem listed in alphabetical order. "Air" starts with "A," so it should come first. That means **G** and **J** are not right. **H** is the only choice that lists the four words in the correct order.

29 B Find the main idea of the poem. (Do you remember this from Mile 13?) The main idea of the poem is that everyone is happy when winter is over and spring has arrived. The poem talks about all of the things that people do because they are happy winter is over. The other three answer choices do not describe what the entire poem is about.

30 F Lines 17 through 20 tell about games people like to play in the spring. If you go back and read these lines, you will find that this is what they are about. The other answer choices are from different parts of the poem. It may help to go back to the poem and read it again after you read the questions.

31 D The joyful people in the poem laugh and sing, so **D** is correct. Lines 21 and 22 talk about the people laughing and singing. The other answer choices are not things that joyful people do in the poem.

32 G At the end of the poem, the children are most likely going to ride bicycles. That makes **G** correct. Riding bikes is a thing to do in spring. All of the other answer choices are things people would do in winter. Would you make a snowball in the spring? Of course not!

33 A Look at the fifth line of this poem. It says, "<u>wander</u> down busy streets." What could that mean? People do not fly kites or get dressed in the street, so **C** and **D** are not correct. Plus, you cannot stay in one place "down the street"! To wander means to walk slowly.

34 H Look at the picture in the question. The picture has grass in it. No one is playing ball, no one is singing, and no one is on the street. That makes **H** the answer.

35 B Read the two lines from the poem in the box. Look at the underlined word, "<u>it's</u>." Do you know what that means? It is a contraction that means, "it is." (Remember that from Mile 7?) If you did not know that, you could still have gotten the answer right. How? Put the answer choices into the sentence. Try **A** first. Does "When it has time for spring" make sense? No, it doesn't. Does "When it is time for spring" make sense? Yes! Try **C** and **D** just to be sure. They don't sound right either. **B** is it!

PRACTICE TEST 2 ANSWERS AND EXPLANATIONS

SHARING

1 **B** Say the word "right" out loud. Now say all the words in the answer choices out loud. Which one rhymes with "right"? It's "bite"! "Seat" and "caught" do not have an "i" sound, and "high" does not end with a "t" sound.

2 **H** This question asks you which line in the poem tells about THINGS. Look at lines 8, 18, 21, and 23, which are the answer choices. Line 21 tells about "books" and "cookies." Those words are nouns, which are things. The other lines talk about actions (which are verbs) or nothing at all.

3 **D** You have to find the line from the poem that BEST describes the poem's main idea. The poem is about sharing. In fact, that's the *name* of the poem! That makes **D** the right answer choice. All of the other answers are talked about in the poem, but only **D** describes what the whole poem is about. The poem is about the fact that sharing is fun and right.

4 **H** Look at the four words in the answer choices. Now figure out which word would come first in alphabetical order. Use the first letter of each word. "F" comes before "M," "S," or "T," so the correct answer is **H.**

5 **C** **C** is correct, because giving ice cream to a friend is an example of sharing. Based on the poem, the narrator would not ask for money, steal a book, or stay home alone to play. The poem is all about sharing, so the narrator would probably like to share the most!

6 **H** Read the end of line 2. The last word is "there." Now look for a word at the end of lines 1, 3, 4, or 5 that is a rhyming word. The words at the end of those lines are "better," "together," "care," and "happier." The only word that rhymes with "there" is "care." That makes **H** correct. None of the other lines in the answer choices end in a word that rhymes with "share."

7 **B** Look at the picture in the question. The two people in the picture are sharing a game. None of the other answer choices except **B** tell about a game. That's why **B** is the best choice.

8 **J** Look at the lines from the poem. "Doesn't" is the contraction for "does not." The contraction for **F** would be "didn't." The contraction for **G** would be "don't." The contraction for **H** would be "won't."

9 **C** The poem is about how good it is to share. The lesson comes from the whole poem, not just one thing mentioned in the poem. That makes **A, B,** and **D** incorrect answer choices. **C** is the best bet.

Peaches Has an Adventure

10 F Do you know the meaning of the word <u>famous</u>? If not, you should look it up in the dictionary for practice! Even if you didn't know what the word meant, try to see which answer choice makes the most sense. The two dogs will be well known because they have found something very special. They are not in trouble, they did not get sent home, and they are not hungry.

11 D Look for the list that shows words from the story listed in alphabetical order. It helps to look at the first letter of each word. "Dinosaur" should come first in the list because it starts with "D." That makes **D** correct because it lists "dinosaur" first. In the other three choices the first word begins with a letter that does not come first alphabetically.

12 F A tall tale is the BEST description of this story. A tall tale is a story that is not true. The story cannot be true because dogs do not talk. The story is not about a famous person, so a biography, **G,** is not right. There are also no ghosts in the story. That leaves **F** as the only answer.

13 C Peaches can be BEST described as serious. She is not lazy, because she runs into the woods. The story does not say she is unhappy. And she is not afraid. That leaves **C** as the best answer choice.

14 G Peaches's master probably learned to listen to his dog. Peaches's master wouldn't listen to Peaches at first, but he learned to trust his dog. Her master is going to want to go back into the woods to find more dinosaur bones. That makes **F** not true. He might spend more time in the museum, **H,** but he did not learn that in the story. And there is no reason for him to be afraid of dinosaurs, **J,** since they are no longer alive.

15 C Look at the sentence in the box. The word "week" is underlined. Sound it out. What is the middle part? It sounds like "ee." Now look at the words in the answer choices. The middle sound of "break" sounds like "a." The middle of "shell" sounds like "e" as in "bell." And the middle part of "fine" sounds like "i" as in "mine." None of those middle sounds is like the middle sound in "week." Only "leak" has a middle sound like "week."

16 G The best place to find more information on dinosaurs would be an encyclopedia. An encyclopedia is where you can look up information about things. A map gives directions. A thesaurus tells you what words have the same meanings as other words. A dictionary gives definitions and spelling information. That's why **G** is the best answer choice.

17 A Look at the time line carefully. Read the events in order. You have to decide what event in the answer choices fits in the third spot. Peaches sees the bone after she goes into the woods but before she has an idea. That makes **A** correct. She never chews on a bone in the story, and she does not become famous, although she might after the story is over.

18 H Peaches wants to show her master the bone because she thinks it is from a monster. Peaches thinks there is a monster loose in the woods. She does not think her master will like the bone. She does not ask him to help carry it. She never says that she wants to become famous. **H** makes the most sense.

Forest Friends

19 D The picture is of a stamp. You have to find the word that has the same end sound as the word "stamp." Look at the answer choices. What word ends in "amp"? It's "camp," making **D** correct! None of the other words ends in "amp." "Berries" ends in an "s," "ground" ends in a "d," and "Jack" ends in a "k."

20 J <u>You're</u> is a contraction for <u>you are</u>. Go back to Mile 7 if you forgot what a contraction is. Try to put the answer choices into the sentence to see if they make sense. For example, try **F**: Does "You is making that up" sound correct? No. Only **J** fits.

21 C Jack sings to the animals because he wants berries for breakfast. In the story Jack says he wants berries for breakfast. He does not always believe his brothers, so **B** cannot be right. The story does not say anything about making the animals angry or not liking berries, so **A** and **D** are also not right.

22 H Look at the picture in the question. Do you see what it is? There is a tent with three pots of berries outside it. Now read the answer choices. Which one describes the picture? The sentences in **F** and **J** do not talk about berries. They are not correct. **G** mentions berries, but it says that Jack did not get any berries. But since all three pots are full, **G** is wrong. **H** is right!

23 A Jack thinks his brothers are playing a joke on him because he knows that animals do not pick berries for people. Jack never mentions that his brothers play mean tricks on him. He never hears his brothers laughing. The story never says that the boys play jokes on each other when they toast marshmallows. Jack tells his brothers that animals do not pick berries for people. That makes **A** the best choice.

24 G Look at the underlined word in the sentence. It is "joke." You have to find the word that rhymes with it. Both "smoke" and "joke" have a long "o" sound in their middles. Both end with a "k" sound. That means they rhyme! None of the other three words has a long "o" sound.

25 D Jack's brothers were singing strange noises while he was telling his story. Read the story again if it helps you. The first paragraph tells you the right answer. The tent was already set up, dinner was over, and they had not gotten the berries yet. That means that none of the other answer choices can be right.

26 G Jack learns that his brothers can play good jokes. Jack already knew that he liked eating berries; he did not learn that in the story. He also knew that telling stories was his favorite part of camping. Those are not lessons he learned in the story! He also knows that animals do not pick berries. Since his brothers played a joke on Jack in this story, he learned a lesson: his brothers play good jokes.

27 B The next time they go camping, Jack will probably try to catch his brothers playing their joke. He wanted to know how they played their trick! He was not mad, so he will not stay home. No one laughed at him, so that is not a good choice.

All Those Insects

28 J Do you know the contraction *haven't*? It stands for *have not,* which makes **J** correct. Remember that the apostrophe usually stands for a letter or two. In this case it stands for the letter "o." The contractions for the other answer choices would be "won't," "isn't," and "aren't."

29 B Look at the picture. It is a door. Now you have to find the answer choice that rhymes with the word "door." Only "four" has the same sounds in the middle and at the end. The other words in the answer choices all end with different sounds.

30 F **F** is the correct answer choice. "Wood" comes from a tree. That's the word for the first space. "Not" is a negative word, like "no." "Knot" is what you tie in your shoelaces. "Would" and "knot" do not make sense in the sentence in the box.

31 D Read paragraph 6 again. It says that social insects are the most <u>remarkable</u> insects. It says bees and wasps are social insects, and that they all have a special job to do. Does that make them "friendly"? Wasps certainly aren't friendly! **A** is wrong. Are they "large" or "hidden"? Not really. "Amazing" and "remarkable" both mean that something is very unusual and interesting.

32 F Scientists probably will be learning about insects for a long time because there are so many to study. It will take a long time to find and study all the many kinds of insects. The fact that they eat many kinds of food would not make insects harder to study. Neither would the fact that they do not live at the South Pole or live in hives.

33 B To find more information on insects, you should use an encyclopedia. A dictionary would help you find out how to spell "insect." An atlas is a book of maps. Newspapers tell about what is happening in the world. **B** is the best answer choice.

34 H Look for the list that shows four words from the story in alphabetical order. Read the first letter of each word. Grasshoppers starts with the letter "g," so it should come first. Only **H** lists grasshoppers first. It's the right answer choice.

35 A Termites sometimes build hives taller than a person. This fact is stated in paragraph 6. The other kinds of insects are talked about in the story, but none of them builds giant hives.

Practice Test 3 Answers and Explanations

A Walk in the Park

1 **C** Look at the sentence in the box. The word "loose" is underlined. You have to find the word in the answer choices that rhymes with it. "Goose" is the only word with the same middle and ending sounds. If you sound out "push," "boss," and "choice," you will find that they sound different than "goose" and "loose."

2 **F** Kevin learns that his father's invention is a useful one. You know this because the other people in the park ask him to make a collar for their dogs. To answer this question, you must think about what Kevin and his father learn in the story. Go through the answer choices one by one. Try **F** first. Kevin's father made the dog collar by himself, so yes, **F** seems right. Check the other answer choices to be sure. **G** isn't true, because Sparky's collar *was* helpful when it got dark! **H** doesn't tell about something that Kevin and his father learned, so it isn't right either. **J** may be true, but the story doesn't tell about playing catch with a dog! **F** is the best answer choice.

3 **D** Dog Park is a special park because dogs can run around freely there, without a leash. It is the newest park in town, so **A** isn't the right answer choice. Only Sparky wore the special collar. Mr. O'Shea built the collar—not the park. That makes **B** and **C** wrong.

4 **H** The word for what is described in the picture is "king." Both "king" and "collar" begin with a hard "c" sound. In the word "know," the "k" is silent, so it doesn't begin with the same sound as "king." "Chop" and "shoe" do not have a hard "c" sound.

5 **A** Mr. O'Shea solved the problem of walking Sparky at night by making a collar with lights on it. The lights allowed him to see Sparky in the dark. That way he always knew where Sparky was. That also meant he could walk him during the day or at night.

6 **F** Look at the sentence in the box. The word "Couldn't" is underlined. "Couldn't" is the contraction for "could not." The contractions for **G** and **H** would be "won't" and "doesn't." There is no contraction for "am not."

7 **D** In the picture the dog is chasing a ball. **D** is the only answer choice that mentions a ball. That makes **D** the best bet.

8 **H** The other people in the Dog Park will probably want lighted collars so they can see their dogs at night too. There is no reason to walk in another park, so **F** is not right. Mr. O'Shea is not building another park, and there is no reason for Kevin to put Sparky on a leash. That makes **G** and **J** wrong too.

9 **A** Mr. O'Shea told Kevin to turn on Sparky's collar when it started to get dark. He says this in the fifth paragraph. All of the other answer choices do happen in the story, but not at the time when it starts to get dark. That is why you have to read each question carefully.

Across the Sky

10 J Say the word "loud." Now look for a word in the answer choices with the same middle and ending sounds. "Proud" has the same sounds in the middle and at the end as "loud." None of the other words ends in a "D" sound.

11 C Look for the list that shows four words from the poem in alphabetical order. It helps to look at the first letter of each word. The words start with "F," "E," "S," and "P." When you put them in order, the "E" word should come first. The "S" word should come last. **C** is the only answer choice that has all four words in correct alphabetical order.

12 J Read lines 6, 10, 14, and 18 again. Look for the line in the poem that shows a person doing an action. In line 18 a person is watching the planes. In line 10 the plane is doing something. Lines 6 and 14 don't really show an action at all. **J** is the right answer choice.

13 B This poem is about airplanes. That means that the narrator is probably interested in planes. The poem does not mention trains, model cars, or cookies, so **A**, **C**, and **D** are not good answer choices.

14 F The picture in the question shows an airplane full of people. You have to pick the answer choice that describes that. The line in **F** talks about an airplane carrying many people. That makes it the best answer choice. The lines in **G**, **H**, and **J** do not describe all the people on the plane.

15 D Look at the sentence in the box. The words "we are" are underlined. You have to pick the correct contraction for them. "We're" is the contraction for "we are." "He'll" means "he will." "Wasn't" means "was not." "There'll" means "there will."

16 H You must find the line that rhymes with line 14. The word at the end of line 14 is "day." Read lines 13, 15, 16, and 18 to find which line ends with a rhyming word. The word at the end of line 16 is "stay." The words at the end of the other lines do not rhyme with "day" and "stay." Always remember to sound words out to see if they rhyme.

17 B In this poem the narrator is watching airplanes. The narrator is on the ground watching planes fly in the sky. He is looking up at a plane, so he cannot be inside one. That makes **A** wrong. He is not watching a movie, so **C** is wrong too. He may go on an adventure later, but that is not talked about in the poem. **D** is incorrect.

18 J Read lines 13 though 16 again. What do they tell you about? They tell about the pilots and the crew of the planes. Now read the questions in the answer choices. **J** fits perfectly. Lines 13 through 16 don't tell about how high the plane flies, where it is going, or what the passengers do.

ALLY'S RACE

19 **B** Ally learns that she has fun racing. Ally doesn't learn that she is scared because she is not scared at the end. **C** has nothing to do with learning. **D** talks about something that happens, not something that Ally learns.

20 **F** Look at the sentence in the box. You have to figure out the meaning of the word "gripped" from the sentence. See which answer choices make the most sense. She would not throw away the wheel, so **G** doesn't seem right. She would not try to hide it, so **H** is probably wrong too. **J** cannot be correct because you cannot think about something tightly! Ally held onto it tightly with her hands because she was afraid.

21 **D** Look for the word in the answer choices with the same middle vowel sound as "snake." Say the word "snake" out loud. The middle sound is a long "a" sound, like the middle vowel sound in "race." The words in **A, B,** and **C** all have the letter "a," in then, but the sound it makes in each word is different.

22 **F** Ally is excited when the race is over because she has finished the race safely and in third place. It was not as scary as she first thought. She is no longer afraid, and she was never tired or bored in the story.

23 **D** Ally was afraid of hitting another go-cart. That makes **D** the right answer. The story mentions in the beginning that Ally is afraid of hitting another car. None of the other answers is something she is afraid of.

24 **H** Ally is very happy because she finished in third place. That changes her mind about entering the next race. **H** is correct. **F** and **G** are not true because her parents never say she has to enter the race and she is not upset over losing. Her legs *do* feel like noodles during the story, but that doesn't change her mind. Ally is excited about finishing in third place, and she wants to race again.

25 **D** In the picture Ally is getting ready to hug her parents. **A** cannot be right because she is not driving anymore. **B** cannot be right because the car has already stopped. **D** is the only answer choice that mentions her parents.

26 **F** Look at the time line carefully. You need to find the event that happens *before she crossed the finish line.* Only **F** fits. Her eyes watered from the wind while she was still racing. That came before her parents congratulated her, she came in third place, and her legs felt like noodles. All of the other events and answer choices happened after the race was over.

27 **B** Before she finishes the race, Ally feels frightened because she is going so fast. She does not want to pass any other carts, so **A** is wrong. She never realizes she is doing well until the race is over, so **D** cannot be right either. **C** does not happen until after the race is over.

FROM VIRGINIA TO THE SOUTH POLE

28 F Look at the drawing of the number four. Say the number out loud. It ends with the "r" sound. That is the same sound as the end of the word "explore." None of the other answer choices ends in the same sound.

29 C Read the two sentences in the box. Try to figure out which words fit in the blank spaces. The "flu" is an illness. "See" means to look at something with your eyes. "Flew" and "sea" are the correct words to use in this example.

30 J The best place to find more information about other people is a biography. Biographies are books about famous people. That means a biography of Admiral Byrd would have a lot of information about him. A dictionary is where you find the meanings and spellings of words. An atlas is a book of maps. A map is a picture that helps you locate places.

31 B If Admiral Byrd had lived longer, he probably would have continued doing research on the South Pole. Byrd was very interested in the South Pole. There was no reason for him to go back to being a sailor or to become afraid of flying. And since he loved to explore, he would probably not want to stop.

32 G "Couldn't" is the contraction for "could not." "Can't" means "cannot." "Didn't" means "did not." "Doesn't" means "does not." **G** is the best answer choice.

33 D Read paragraph 2 again. Do you see the sentence that has the word "skilled" underlined? If you don't know what the word "skilled" means, try to fit the answer choices in the sentence. Only "talented," **D**, sounds right. None of the other three answers makes sense if you put them into the sentence instead of "skilled."

34 H Admiral Byrd was determined and daring. "Determined" means doing something no matter what stands in the way. "Daring" means willing to do something no one has ever done before. Those words describe him better than the words in the other choices.

35 C After he flew over the North Pole, Admiral Byrd explored the South Pole. That makes **C** correct. The other three answer choices list events that happened *before* he flew over the North Pole.

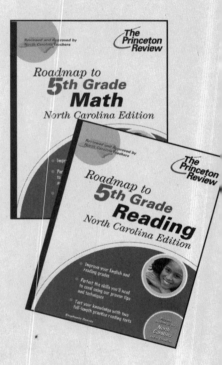